Stalin's Genocides

Stalin's Genocides

Norman M. Naimark

PRINCETON UNIVERSITY PRESS
Princeton & Oxford

Published by Princeton University Press, 41 William Street,
Princeton, New Jersey 08540

In the United Kingdom: Princeton University Press,
6 Oxford Street, Woodstock, Oxfordshire OX20 1TW

press.princeton.edu

Fourth printing, and first paperback printing, 2012
Paperback ISBN 978-0-691-15238-7

THE LIBRARY OF CONGRESS HAS CATALOGED THE CLOTH EDITION
OF THIS BOOK AS FOLLOWS

Naimark, Norman M.
Stalin's genocides / Norman M. Naimark.
p. cm. — (Human rights and crimes against humanity)
Includes bibliographical references and index.
ISBN 978-0-691-14784-0 (hardcover : alk. paper)
1. Genocide—Soviet Union—History. 2. Mass murder—
Soviet Union—History. 3. Political purges—Soviet Union—History.
4. Political persecution—Soviet Union—History. 5. Stalin, Joseph,
1879–1953. 6. Soviet Union—Politics and government—1917–1936.
7. Soviet Union—Politics and government—1936–1953. 8. Human
rights—Soviet Union—History. 9. International law—Soviet Union—
History.10. Soviet Union—History—1925–1953. I. Title.
DK268.4.N35 2010   947.084'2—dc22
2010019063

British Library Cataloging-in-Publication Data is available

This book has been composed in Bauer Bodoni

Printed on acid-free paper. ∞

Printed in the United States of America

7   9   10   8

CONTENTS

Acknowledgments

This study grew out of a long-term preoccupation with the history of genocide and the way Stalin and his crimes should be viewed in the context of that history. I explored some of these problems at a series of conferences and symposia that helped develop my views. I should mention in particular the Mellon Foundation Sawyer Seminar Series on Mass Killing at the Center for Advanced Study on the Behavioral Sciences at Stanford, which I organized together with Ronald G. Suny; a conference on "Totalitarianism" sponsored by *Telos* and organized by Russell Berman at Stanford; and a conference in honor of Robert Conquest, held at the American Enterprise Institute and organized by Paul Hollander. I am also beholden to those colleagues who commented on this work at a "Hitler-Stalin Workshop" at Yale, chaired by Timothy Snyder, and at the Workshop of Turkish and Armenian Scholars (WATS) held at Berkeley and led by Gerard Libaridian. The comments and criticisms of participants at these conferences and meetings proved extremely helpful in sharpening my views of Stalin and the genocide question. Several published essays resulted from these talks and papers, and the present book is built on the arguments that are contained in them.[1]

Similarly, I benefited enormously from the critiques of the draft manuscript by a number of distinguished scholars: Paul Gregory, Hiroaki Kuromiya, David Shearer, Robert Service, Yuri Slezkine, Ronald Suny, Amir Weiner, and Eric Weitz. The readers at Princeton University Press, Jan T. Gross and Lynne Viola, also provided valuable comments and suggestions. Throughout my professional life, I have had the remarkably good fortune of learning from my friends and colleagues in the field. This book, in particular, owes a lot to the input of these readers. Their criticisms, observations, and corrections helped me avoid some pretty bad mistakes and pointed out holes in my argument. They gave me additional sources to read and new perspectives to include. At the same time, I have dug in my heels on a number of issues where many of my friends thought differently. That familiar disclaimer works in this case in spades: I alone am responsible for the views that are expressed in this book.

I also am beholden to my friend and colleague Amir Eshel, director of the Forum for Contemporary Europe at Stanford's Freeman-Spogli Institute, for having helped arrange the lecture at Suhrkamp in Berlin, which was the inspiration for actually writing a small book on Stalin. Thomas Sparr at Suhrkamp has been a generous and encouraging editor and a strong advocate of the Stanford-Suhrkamp lecture program. Brigitta van Rheinberg at

Princeton University Press has been as supportive and understanding an editor as any author could hope for.

I have also had some very helpful research assistants at Stanford, who have not only chased down sources but also shared their views of the subject with me. None has been more important to the completion of this project than Valentin Bolotnyy, who has become a real friend in the process of doing this work. As usual, the archivists and staff of the invaluable Hoover Institute Archives have been wonderfully helpful and patient with my requests. My gratitude to Kathryn Ward for her close reading of the book's page proofs.

Finally, I would like to thank my wife, Katherine Jolluck, my son, Ben, and my daughters, Anna and Sarah. The darkness that inevitably comes from immersing myself in Stalinism lifts immediately when encountering my joyful family. There is an added benefit in that Katherine is an accomplished historian and superb editor, who reads critically everything I write. This book is dedicated with gratitude and love to her.

Stalin's Genocides

INTRODUCTION

This short book—really an extended essay—is intended to argue that Stalin's mass killings of the 1930s should be classified as "genocide." This argument is made more difficult by the fact that there was no single act of genocide in the Soviet case, but rather a series of interrelated attacks on "class enemies" and "enemies of the people," metonyms for diverse alleged opponents of the Soviet state. Episodes of mass killing also took a variety of forms, some involving mass executions, others exile in special settlements and camps of the Gulag, where many hundreds of thousands died from the unusually harsh character of arrest, internment, and interrogation, on the one hand, and hellish conditions of transport, housing, sustenance, and forced labor, on the other.

The social and national categories of the supposed enemies of the USSR changed and shifted over time; the justifications for the assaults on groups of Soviet citizens (and foreigners in the Soviet Union) were similarly labile. Yet Stalin and his lieutenants connected these genocidal attacks to the tenets of Marxism-Leninism-Stalinism and used similar police, judicial, and extrajudicial means of implementing them. Both Soviet party and state institutions were involved, as Stalin applied the impressive instruments of exerting power and control created by the Bolshevik revolution to strike at his opponents and potential opponents, real and—for the greatest part—imagined. As the result of Stalin's rule in the 1930s and early 1940s, many millions of innocent people were shot, starved to death, or died in detention and exile. It is long since time to consider this story an important chapter in the history of genocide.

There are a number of legitimate scholarly and even moral inhibitions in making this kind of argument, not the least important of which is the understandable reticence—pronounced among both scholars and journalists—to apply an appellation designed primarily to describe the Holocaust, the mass murder of the Jews by the Nazis, to the murder of Soviet citizens in the 1930s. In particular, German and Jewish scholars of the Holocaust will sometimes insist that the Nazi murder of nearly six million Jews was an event of singular historical meaning that cannot be fruitfully compared with other episodes of mass murder in the modern era. The combination of Hitler's murderous racism and traditional Christian anti-Semitic motifs make Nazi crimes, in the mind of many scholars, a unique genocidal undertaking.[1] But even this question becomes more complicated when one takes into account what could be considered Nazi genocidal campaigns against gypsies (Roma and Sinti), homosexuals, and the mentally disabled, not to mention Soviet prisoners of war, Poles, and others.

Related to this issue is the fact that the December 1948 United Nations Convention on the Prevention and Punishment of Genocide focuses on the murder of ethnic, national, racial, and religious groups and excludes—though not explicitly—social and political groups, which were, after all, the main victims of Stalin's murderous campaigns. Some scholars isolate the Ukrainian killer famine of 1932–33 or the forced deportations of the so-called punished peoples in 1944 to support a claim of genocide against Stalin. Others point to the "Katyn forest massacre" of twenty-two thousand Polish army officers and government officials in the early spring of 1940 as an emblematic case of Stalinist genocide. But categorizing just these discrete murderous events as genocide, while leaving out others, tends to gloss over the genocidal character of the Soviet regime in the 1930s, which killed systematically rather than episodically.

Another objection to including Stalinist mass killings in the concept of genocide has to do with the special character of ethnic and national identity when thinking about the "human race." Humanity is comprised of a marvelous diversity of peoples, each of whose distinct character, even if "imagined," in the famous formulation of Benedict Anderson, deserves special protection. As we will see, the development of the concept of genocide itself was closely tied to this idea. Yet the U.N. Genocide Convention also protects religious groups, despite the fact that their essentially ascriptive nature does not carry the same valence as ethnic and national groups. Jews and Armenians were killed as peoples, not as religious groups, though religion was used as a marker of ethnicity, much as it was in the case of Serb attacks on Bosnian Muslims in the 1990s. But the obligation of protecting ethnic and national groups, as well as religious and racial ones, from mass murder should not obviate the need to protect political and social groups from the same horrendous crime, especially when the Soviet Union insisted that these groups not be included in the Genocide Convention. Certainly the victims and their progeny would have difficulty understanding the moral, ethical, and legal differences—not to mention historical distinctions—between one form of mass murder and another.

At the same time many observers think that the concept of genocide would lose its historical and legal salience, would in some senses be "cheapened," by broadening the potential categories of victims to include social and political groups. It is certainly the case that the term is used imprecisely and irresponsibly by diverse, sometimes loosely defined, groups of people claiming genocide victim status. But it is the very enormity of the crime of systematic mass murder—intentionally perpetrated by the political elite of a state against a targeted group within the borders of or outside the state—that should distinguish genocide from other forms of mass killing, like pogroms, massacres, and terrorist bombings. To include the planned mass elimination of social and political groups in the definition of genocide can help make our understanding of the phenomenon more robust rather than diminish its historical usefulness. Often in episodes of genocide—we see this particularly clearly in the case of the Ukrainian killer famine of 1932–1933—social and national/ethnic categories overlap. Sometimes, as in the case of the Soviet attack against so-called kulaks, social and political categories of victims were "ethnicized" as a way to make the attack on their existence more comprehensible to the society and state. Genocide as a product of communist societies—Stalinist Russia, Mao's China, and Pol Pot's Cambodia—where millions of these country's own citizens were killed in campaigns of mass murder, can and should be thought about alongside analogous cases of genocide perpetrated against minority peoples.

For decades, Cold War politics in academia (meaning, in particular, anti–Cold War politics) also militated against an open consideration of the genocide question in the context of Stalin and Stalinism. This continues to have some relevance to our understanding of the Soviet Union even today. Because Stalin killed in the name of the higher ideals of socialism and human progress, it is sometimes argued, his cannot be equated with the base motives of history's other twentieth-century genocidaires, who killed for no other reason than the perceived "otherness" of ethnic or religious groups, and, in Hitler's case, for a racial dystopia that could appeal to few except the Germans. In assessing Stalin's motivations for overseeing the mass killing of so many millions of Soviet citizens in the 1930s, historians can sometimes seem anxious to find a plausible rationale for him to have done so, whether it be the breakneck program to modernize the country, the need to provide heavy industry with investment capital and agriculture with technological improvements, the protection of the Soviet Union from the threat of invasion by its enemies, most notably Poland, Germany, and Japan, the presence of potential terrorists in the population out to kill Stalin and his confederates, and/or the nefarious influence of Trotsky and his Fourth International on the Soviet elite.

In the recent literature on Stalin's crimes, Viacheslav Molotov's memories in conversation with Feliks Chuev, recorded some thirty-five years after the events, are frequently used to explain the purges and the killing:

> 1937 was necessary. If you take into account that after the revolution we hacked to the right and to the left, and achieved victory, but the remnants of enemies of various viewpoints continued to exist, and in face of the growing danger of fascist aggression they could unite. We were obliged in 1937 to make sure that at the time of war we would not have a fifth column. . . . Of course, it's sad and regrettable about such people [who were innocent], but I believe that the terror that was carried out at the end of the 1930s was necessary. . . . Stalin, in my opinion, conducted absolutely the right policy; so what if extra heads fell, there would be no vacillation in the time of war and after the war.

Even in his old age, after having seen his wife, Polina Zhemchuzhina, hauled off into exile in Kazakhstan on trumped-up charges, Molotov asserted that the purges were not just necessary but were directed against guilty comrades, though he admitted that injustices were inevitably involved. The rehabilitations that occurred in the post-Stalin period were nothing more than "fashionable falsifications."[2]

The notion that the terrible mass killing of the 1930s was carried out in anticipation of the coming conflagration and, indeed, was crucial in assuring the eventual Soviet victory in the "Great Fatherland War" over the Nazis fits not just Molotov's and other Stalinists' aphoristic injunctions that "an omelette cannot be made without breaking some eggs" and that "forests cannot be cleared without chips flying"—in short, that lives had to be sacrificed to achieve the greater gains of Soviet-style socialism. Many scholars in Russia and the West believe that Stalin prepared for war by carrying out dekulakization, purges, and campaigns against alleged internal enemies, social, political, and national. Even the mass purges of the Soviet armed forces, of the intelligence services, and of foreign communists, which one might assume would clearly damage Stalin's chances of winning an impending war by eliminating those most knowledgeable about fighting it, are thought to be rational preparations for the coming conflict.[3] Because Stalin won the war, the argument goes—*post hoc ergo propter hoc* (after this, therefore because of this)—these supposed preparations during the 1930s, no matter how brutal, violent, and counterproductive, can be justified and therefore cannot be classified as genocide, the "crime of crimes" in international jurisprudence, which can have no justification.

The combination of the Soviet victory in the Second World War, the place of honor accorded Stalin in the reconstruction of the world order after 1945, and the secretiveness of the Soviet regime kept the extent and intensity of Soviet mass killing from world attention, not to mention from the Russian public. Now that many archives of the Soviet period are accessible and some Russians, including most recently the president of the Russian Federation, Dmitri Medvedev, are asking fundamental questions about the murderousness of the Stalinist regime, the genocide question can and should be approached with new openness. A majority of Russians continue to hold Stalin in high esteem, despite their knowledge of the killing fields that contain the mass graves of their forebears. To establish the contours of genocide is crucial for the country's own self-understanding and future. Moreover, relations with Ukrainians, the Baltic peoples, Poles, Chechens, and Crimean Tatars, all of whom claim to one extent or another to be the victims of Stalinist genocide, can improve only if the Russians openly acknowledge and conscientiously investigate the crimes of the past. Genocide lives in historical memory and, unrecognized—as we know from the case of the Turkish government and the Armenian genocide of 1915—distorts and disrupts relations between peoples and nations. Scholars of the Soviet past, here and there, are obliged to face genocide and its consequences squarely.

The book begins with a discussion of the issues surrounding the use of the term genocide itself. I argue that there are good reasons to think about and apply the U.N. Convention on the Prevention and Punishment of the Crime of Genocide in a broader and more flexible pattern of cases than has sometimes been done in the scholarly literature. This is especially important in examining Stalinist cases since the Soviet Union and its allies helped to formulate the definition of genocide by essentially vetoing the inclusion of social and political groups, which had been included in virtually all of the early drafts of the U.N. genocide convention. Also, the international courts have moved in the direction of a broader understanding of genocide. A good example is the 2004 judgment of the International Criminal Tribunal for the former Yugoslavia (ICTY) in the case of Radoslav Krstić, which ruled that the Bosnian Serbs' mass execution of nearly eight thousand Bosnian Muslim men and boys in Srebrenica in July 1995 constituted genocide. That same court concluded in an appeal of the case that an incident of mass killing like Srebrenica can be designated as genocide, even without having been able to convict any of the perpetrators of genocide. In February 2007 the International Court of Justice (ICJ), also in The Hague, similarly ruled that Srebrenica was a case of genocide in a ruling on a suit, otherwise dismissed, that was filed by the government of Bosnia-Herzegovina against Serbia.

Chapter 2 turns to a consideration of the making of Stalin as a genocidaire. Here, as elsewhere in this study, I rely heavily on some of the best biographies of Stalin that have recently been published, by Robert Service, Hiroaki Kuromiya, Dimitri Volkogonov, Simon Sebag Montefiore, Donald Rayfield, Miklos Kun, and Ronald G. Suny (in manuscript), among others, as well as some memoirs and unpublished works about Stalin's life. The third, fourth, and fifth chapters of the book examine concrete episodes of mass killing in the 1930s that made up the foundation of Stalin's genocidal enterprise: dekulakization in 1929–31, the Ukrainian famine in 1932–33, and the murderous campaigns against non-Russian nationalities that stretched from 1934 into the war. Chapter 6 surveys the Great Terror in 1937–38. There is by now a huge literature on all of these subjects; much of the most recent scholarship is based on the opening of important archival collections and the publication of seminal documents in Russia and in the West. In this connection, this book owes a great debt to the substantial international community of historians of the Soviet Union, who have done a remarkable job of researching the dark corners of the Stalinist period.

The goal of these chapters on mass killing in the 1930s and early 1940s is to emphasize some of the most important definitional characteristics of genocide: the motives of the perpetrators; the line of command from the "boss" (*khoziain*) or the "warrior-leader" (*vozhd'*)— Stalin—to the executors of his policies; and the attempt to eliminate all or part of these groups of victims, as groups. These questions of intent, motive, and line of command have dominated the cases brought against the perpetrators in the wars in the Balkans and Sub-Saharan Africa in the ICTY in The Hague and the International Criminal Tribunal for Rwanda (ICTR) in Arusha, and they are the most important in assessing the culpability of Stalin and his regime for genocide in the 1930s. But also relevant are cases of alleged genocide that have been brought before the judicial systems of the post-Soviet Baltic states and of several Latin American countries, most notably Argentina.

The final chapter of the book surveys the problem of comparing Nazi and Soviet crimes. Implicit in any evaluation of Stalin's mass killing of the 1930s is our knowledge and understanding of the horrors of the Holocaust. Nothing in history can quite capture the shock to the human system of the image of hundreds of thousands of naked and helpless men and women, including the very old and the very young, being systematically gassed and then incinerated in the ovens of Nazi crematoria. Many historians believe that Hitler's ultimate goal was to kill all of the world's Jews, which would represent unprecedented and unmatched criminal intent. Yet Stalin's responsibility for the killing of some fifteen to twenty million people carries its own horrific weight, in part because it was done in the name of one of the most influential and purportedly progressive political ideologies of modern times, communism.

Before proceeding, a word about the number of Stalinist victims is in order. Since 1990 a large number of Soviet documents have been declassified and made available to researchers by the Russian archival service. Especially reports from the OGPU and NKVD—the Soviet security police organizations —list in striking detail and with extraordinary completeness the numbers of arrested, executed, and deported in the period under consideration. But these numbers need to be used very carefully, and in no way do they represent the final word on how many Soviet citizens were "repressed" in the 1930s and how many were killed. The fact that the columns of numbers always add up and that the numbers themselves are always given to the last digit—496,460 deported Chechens and Ingush, for example, or 1,803,392 dekulakized peasants in 1931–32—leads one to believe that this impossible accuracy may reflect deeper problems with the veracity of the numbers.

Sometimes the incentive of the police and judicial bureaucrats was to ratchet up the numbers of arrested and executed, so that their superiors—Stalin and particularly his OGPU/NKVD chiefs, Yagoda, Yezhov, and Beria—would be pleased with the results. More often, their incentive was to underreport or not to report at all, especially when it came to "extraneous" deaths in the Gulag system, including the special settlements, and in the case of famine or dekulakization. In considering the numbers of Soviet citizens killed in the Gulag, Alexander Yakovlev, who was head of a commission to investigate Stalinist mass killings and had unusual access to a wide spectrum of archival sources, warns against accepting the NKVD numbers as gospel. He states point-blank that "these [NKVD figures] are false. . . . They do not take account of the number of people confined in the internal prisons of the NKVD, and those prisons were jammed packed. They do not break down the mortality rates in camps for political prisoners, and they ignore the number of arrested peasants and deported peoples."[4] In any case, the false precision of the NKVD data, plus the constantly shifting political agendas of Stalin's chief repressive agencies, should be enough to insert a note of skepticism into the confident use of NKVD numbers by contemporary historians.

The observer needs to approach the history of Stalinist mass killing from the early 1930s until the war with several warning signals in mind. There is the problem of conflating political purges with dekulakization, the forced deportation of nations with the elimination of "asocials" in Order 00447, the shooting of Polish officers in 1940 with the trials and execution of Soviet military officers in 1938, and all of these "episodes" in the history of the period with each other. At the same time, scholars have been wont to miss the genocidal characteristics of Stalin's rule in this period by making excessively rigid distinctions between these events. Also, not every one of these cases can be considered genocide, which required a certain level of murderous premeditation on the part of Stalin and his government and an intention to attack the group as a whole by destroying a significant part of it. This was not everywhere and always the case in the 1930s and early 1940s; some episodes bear more clearly than others the taint of genocide. Of course, intention is very difficult to demonstrate, even with improved documentation and access to archives in Russia. Stalin and his lieutenants frequently used forced deportation to punish one group or another within the Soviet population for alleged crimes. Forced deportation is clearly a "crime against humanity," but the results can sometimes be considered "genocidal," meaning "like genocide," but not necessarily with the same jurisprudential implications that come from labelling discrete episodes "genocide." Altogether, these kinds of distinctions are tricky and elusive. Yet, they are impor-

tant in understanding the murderous character of Stalin's
rule. In short, there are scholarly dangers in conflating
these episodes of mass killing, but also in separating them
too rigidly.

To place Stalin at the center of the genocide question
is not meant as a way of excluding social, political, economic, and ideological determinants of mass killing in the
Soviet Union in the 1930s. The Soviet Union in the Stalinist period was not simply a personal dictatorship, though
it was also that. A vast network of state organizations had
to be mobilized to seize and kill that many people, most
prominent among them the police, especially the political
police. The "accomplices of genocide"—in a legal as well
as historical sense—had to number in the tens of thousands. Yet once Stalin died, mass killing ceased altogether
in the Soviet Union. Before Stalin's dictatorship, this study
argues, one should not use the appellation of genocide for
the mass killing that took place, despite its horrific character, especially during the Civil War of 1918–21. Stalin
made a huge difference, and it is Stalin's role in mass killing that is essential in understanding the genocidal character of his regime.

1 THE GENOCIDE ISSUE

The specific language of the U.N. Convention on the Prevention and Punishment of the Crime of Genocide of December 1948 is frequently cited as the reason why Stalin's crimes cannot be considered genocide. However, if one looks at the history of the convention itself, there are good reasons to think more flexibly about the document's meaning. The Polish Jewish lawyer Raphael Lemkin, who coined the term "genocide" during World War II, first came up with a definition of what he then called "barbarism" in 1933 in a proposal to the League of Nations: "Whosoever, out of hatred towards a racial, religious or social collectivity, or with a view of the extermination thereof, undertakes a punishable action against the life, bodily integrity, liberty, dignity or economic existence of a person belonging to such a collectivity, is liable, for the crime of barbarity." Lemkin added: "Whosoever, either out of hatred towards a racial, religious or social collectivity, or with a view to the extermination thereof, destroys its cultural or artistic works will be liable for the crime of vandalism."[1]

After fleeing Poland from the Nazis in 1940 and landing in the United States, Lemkin continued his search for an international legal statute against mass killing, extermination, and "vandalism." He first developed his definition of the new term "genocide" in the document collection *Axis Rule in Occupied Europe*, which he published as a consultant for the War Department in 1944. He had been searching for the right word to describe the horrors of mass murder, expulsion, and oppression, one that would jolt the consciousness of his readers, and, clearly, he was sure that he had found it: "The practices of extermination of nations and ethnic groups as carried out by the invaders [the Nazis] is called by the author 'genocide,' a term deriving from the Greek work *genos* (tribe, race) and the Latin *cide* (by way of analogy, see homicide, fratricide)."[2]

We are not certain why Lemkin dropped crimes against social or political entities (versus religious, racial, or ethnic ones) from his 1944 book. In all likelihood, he did so primarily to emphasize the particular evil of Nazi racial attacks on Jews, Poles, and others. No doubt, he also wanted to avoid any trouble that his government-sponsored publication might elicit from the Soviet Union, whose participation in the anti-Hitler alliance was particularly valued at this point in Washington. Until the war was won, the American president and his closest advisors tabled questions about the reliability of their Moscow ally. The press and the public lauded the accomplishments of "Uncle Joe" and the gallant fighting men and women of the Red Army, while few objections were raised about the Soviet Union's hostile attitudes toward the Poles, including the massacre of Polish officers at Katyn.[3] Even more important, Roosevelt was planning for a postwar order that would see the creation of a "United Nations" based on a condominium of Soviet and American interests, in particular, even to the point of marginalizing his "imperial" British ally. In this atmosphere, it is not surprising that Lemkin did not insist on maintaining social and political groups in his definition of genocide. Sometimes, however, contemporary scholars overlook the fact that Lemkin continued to advocate a broad and flexible view of genocide, considering many different kinds of cases within the purview of the term, including premodern as well as modern episodes, and suggesting that genocide often took place in different forms, some more or less murderous. In the early 1950s he explicitly included Soviet crimes in his conception of genocide, but he did so rather unsystematically and for transparently political purposes.[4]

After the war, Lemkin tirelessly lobbied for his new definition of genocide in the press and at the Nuremberg trials, which began in the late fall of 1946.[5] He was only partially successful at Nuremberg. Genocide was mentioned several times in the course of the trials, but it was left out of the final pronouncement of the tribunal. In fact, the justices at Nuremberg were much more interested in the condemnation of the Nazis as aggressors in the international system than they were in condemning the mass murder of the Jews. Even at that, the goal was to expose the evil triad of Nazism–militarism–economic imperialism even more than to put on trial war criminals per se and explore their motivations.[6]

At Nuremberg, the Soviets pressed their interests, initially developed in the late 1930s, in using international law

as a means of condemning fascism and Nazism, while seeking to prevent their recurrence. They saw the tribunal as
presenting an opportunity to punish the perpetrators of the
war of aggression and crimes against their own population
and that of their allies, especially the Poles. Already in December 1943 in Ukraine, the Soviets prosecuted a number
of Germans and a Russian collaborator—and, in absentia,
the leaders of the German state and army—for "methodi-
cally striving for the extermination of the Slavic peoples."[7]

Yet the historian does not gain much confidence in Soviet motives at Nuremberg from the fact that almost all
of the dramatis personae of the Soviet delegation were involved in the Moscow show trials of the period 1936–38.
These included General I. Nikitichenko, a presiding judge
in the Zinoviev trial in 1937 and the Soviet prosecutor
and chief judge at Nuremberg, and A. Vyshinskii, the chief
prosecutor of the Moscow show trials. After having demonstrated his worth as a vicious and unrelenting attack
dog of Stalin's during the Moscow trials, where he abused
the defendants and shouted down their attempts to clear
themselves of impossible charges, Vyshinskii was deputy
foreign minister in 1946 during the Nuremberg trials and
head of a secret special commission on Nuremberg that reported directly to Molotov and Stalin. The main job of the
commission, according to Arkady Vaksberg, was to make
sure that there was no public discussion of Nazi–Soviet
relations (not to mention cooperation!) during the period
of the pact, 1939–41. The Soviet government was especially concerned that the secret protocols of the Nazi–Soviet Pact were not mentioned at all.[8]

Apparently, Stalin and the Soviets were disappointed that Nuremberg did not prove as "successful" as their very own Moscow show trials in highlighting the superiority of the Soviet system and demonstrating the perfidy of its enemies. There was no didactic international condemnation of the accused; no uniform death sentences for everyone on the dock; and little attention by world public opinion to the special heroism and suffering of the Soviet people. Sovinformburo (the Soviet state news agency) reported back to Stalin from Nuremberg that Soviet jurists, journalists, and public figures at the trial took a decidedly back-row seat to their Western counterparts in the presentation of the trials to world public opinion. The Soviet representatives at the trial were also disappointed that there were no serious efforts at Nuremberg itself to produce a convention against genocide. From their perspective, the Soviet peoples were the main victims of the racism and imperialism of Nazi Germany and deserved protection against a resurgent Germany through a genocide convention.

In part as a result of their negative reading of Nuremberg, the Soviets showed no interest in later proposals at the United Nations to set up a permanent tribunal to deal with the crime of genocide. Instead, the Soviets insisted that domestic courts in the country where the crime was committed be responsible for trying those accused of genocide.[9] Moreover, an international tribunal, stated Aron Trainin, the Soviets' leading specialist on international law, "under certain circumstances can turn out to provide reasons for unjustifiable interference in the internal life, in the justice system of individual states."[10]

The Soviets were also dismayed at Nuremberg that the German defense attorneys had found the opportunity to bring up alleged Soviet crimes committed during the war—and especially those associated with the period of the Nazi–Soviet Pact—despite a "gentleman's agreement" with Western jurists that the Germans would not be allowed to mention supposed Allied crimes in defense of their clients on the dock. Even if the Western allies broke this agreement toward the end of the proceedings, the Soviets were also able to use the Nuremberg proceedings to perpetuate the myth that the Nazis were responsible for shooting the twenty-two thousand Polish officers and government officials whom Stalin and Beria ordered to be executed by the NKVD in 1940. The Western judges never challenged this shameful subterfuge, though the indictment against the Nazis for the killing was eventually dropped. As Churchill wrote in his memoirs: "It was decided by the victorious governments concerned that the issue should be avoided, and the crime of Katyn was never probed in detail."[11]

After the conclusion of the Nuremberg trials of the major Nazi war criminals, Lemkin lobbied energetically at the newly constituted United Nations for the introduction of an international convention against genocide. More important to its ultimate success, of course, was the determination of the Great Powers, including the Soviet Union, to come to terms with the potential of mass murder of the sort perpetrated by the Nazis in Europe during the war. The first move in this direction was the passage—without debate—of General Assembly resolution 96 (I) on December 11, 1946. The resolution condemned genocide "as a crime under international law . . . whether it is committed on religious, racial, *political or any other ground*" and charged the Economic and Social Council with drawing up a draft convention on the crime of genocide to be presented to the General Assembly.[12] In July 1947 the Secretariat of the United Nations presented a draft of the convention that also sought "to prevent the destruction of racial, national, linguistic, religious *or political groups of human beings.*"[13] Further work on the draft produced a series of additional revisions. As amended by the United States, it included the phrase "on grounds of national or racial origin or religious *or political belief.*" China added "*or political opinion*" instead of "political belief."[14]

All of the early drafts of the genocide convention, including the initial U.N. Secretariat draft of May 1947, included political groups in their definition. The Soviets, the Poles, and even some noncommunist members of the committees and drafting commissions objected. "Political groups," the Soviets insisted, "were entirely out of place in a scientific definition of genocide, and their inclusion would weaken the convention and hinder the fight against genocide." The Polish delegate argued that the United Nations should oppose the extermination of groups of people for their political beliefs, like the mass shooting and killing of (left-wing) "hostages" in Spain, Greece, and elsewhere. But genocide was about mass murder of peoples, as happened to the Poles, the Russians, and the Jews at the hands of the Nazis during the war.[15] The Soviets were so insistent on this point that they urged the inclusion of language in the convention that specifically referred to the fact

that genocide "was organically bound up with fascism-
nazism and other similar race theories which preach racial and national hatred, the domination of the so-called
higher races and the extermination of the so-called lower
races."[10]

The Soviet delegation and its allies were not the only
ones who insisted that political and social groups be left
out of the convention. According to the *New York Times*,
countries like Argentina, Brazil, the Dominican Republic,
Iran, and South Africa were worried that they could be
accused of genocide if they fought against domestic political insurgencies by revolutionary groups. Thus the Soviets
and their right-wing political opponents joined forces in
the United Nations on the genocide issue. Other observers thought that the United Nations would be obligated to
defend Francisco Franco in Spain or even Stalin himself
against potential political revolts if the protection of "political groups" was included in the convention.[17]

Interestingly, Soviet proposals for the genocide convention were not confined to purely "biological" categories.
They proposed that the convention include what they
called "national-cultural genocide," using the following
language. "Under genocide in the present convention we
also understand all of the premeditated actions taken with
the intention of destroying the language, religion, or culture of any national, racial, or religious group." Among
the prohibitions included in the Soviet proposal was "the
destruction of libraries, museums, schools, historical
monuments, buildings used by religious groups, or other
cultural buildings and objects of culture used by such

groups."[18] Here, too, it is clear that the Soviets were think-ing about the Nazis and the terrible destruction wrought on churches, museums, and monuments in Soviet terri-tory, not about their own similar crimes perpetrated in the northern Caucasus, among other places. The United States and its "satellites" (in the words of one Soviet scholar) successfully blocked the Soviet initiative because of American concerns about being indicted for racism and the repression of native cultures at home.

The Soviets did not get "national-cultural genocide" included in the convention, but on the issue of political groups they did in the end wear down the Sixth Com-mittee, in charge of the comprehensive redactions of the convention. A compromise was reached for the purpose of achieving unanimous approval of the convention. "It was for that reason," the American delegate stated, "that it had agreed to the omission of political groups among the groups to be protected by the convention."[19] In the name of getting the convention passed at this point, Lemkin and a number of Jewish groups also lobbied against including "political groups" in its language.[20] As a consequence, the final genocide convention, unanimously adopted by the U.N. General Assembly on December 9, 1948, with Lem-kin in the gallery, famously defined genocide as a variety of "acts committed with the intent to destroy, in whole or in part, a national, ethnical, racial or religious group, as such."

What this brief rendition of the origins of our use of "genocide" makes clear is that the Soviet Union and its al-lies in the United Nations eliminated any social, economic, or political groups from the genocide convention—and, I would add, made it very difficult for scholars to talk about genocide as a product of the Soviet system. The Soviets made the self-serving argument, both in the U.N. committees and in contemporary scholarly works on the subject, that social and political groups were too fluid and too difficult to define for them to be included in the convention.[21] At the same time, in many cases of Stalinist mass killing, the Soviet leaders tended to create just such categories in their own rhetoric and by their own actions. In Stalinist lore, the more than thirty thousand "kulaks" who were shot and the two million who were deported to the Far North, Siberia, and Central Asia during collectivization and after constituted an allegedly identifiable social and political category of rich peasants, in contrast to poor and middle peasants. In fact, this was an invented group of opponents and alleged opponents of collectivization. In the history of genocide, writes Mark Levene, not enough attention has been paid to the ways "a perpetrator can conceive a group as an organized collectivity in spite of itself." In some ways, this was as true of the "Jews," especially fully assimilated German Jews, who were targeted for elimination by the Nazis, as it was of the "kulaks."[22]

Since the fall of the Soviet Union and the independence of the Baltic states, the legal questions regarding Stalin and genocide have taken a decidedly contemporary turn. In their desire to bring to justice perpetrators of crimes against their peoples, Estonia, Latvia, and Lithuania passed their own national laws on genocide, which, though deriving from the 1948 U.N. convention and its subsequent legal history, have broadened the definition

of genocide to include specific crimes perpetrated in the
Baltic region such as forced deportation and the execution of groups of resisters and their supporters. As a result, numbers of alleged Soviet perpetrators of crimes
against the Baltic peoples have been indicted, tried, and,
in some cases, convicted of genocide. These crimes include the NKVD murder and deportation of citizens of
Latvia, Lithuania, and Estonia during the occupation
period, 1940–41. They also include crimes committed
during the reconquest of these countries after World War
II; the NKVD's brutal attacks in 1944–45 on the "forest
brethren" (local resistance groups) and their supporters
in the population; and dekulakization, deportation, and
campaigns against "enemies of the people" and "nationalists" primarily in the period 1948–49, during the collectivization drive in the Baltic states. Those who were
convicted, both Balts and Russians, were essentially cogs
in the Stalinist repressive regime, though often active and
murderous cogs. Interestingly, as far as I know these are
the first and only servants of the Stalinist state to have
stood trial and been convicted for "crimes against humanity" or genocide perpetrated anywhere in the former
Soviet Union.[23]

A number of important insights into the problem of
Soviet genocide are illuminated by the evolution of the
law in the Baltic cases, despite their partly politicized origins.[24] For example, the legal codes in the Baltic states recognize that it is often difficult to prove the intention of the
perpetrator, in this case Stalin, to commit mass murder.
Was there intent to kill so many Balts during the periods
of occupation and reconquest? The courts in the region

conclude—using precedents in international law—that intent can be deduced from the actual events themselves, how many died, and how organized the actions were. The courts note in addition that the atmospherics of the crime are also important: whether the acts of arrest and deportation were conducted according to standard legal procedures at the time, whether they were surrounded by hateful language and demeanor, and whether there was gratuitous brutality during the process. Much like first-degree murder, premeditation and intent in genocide are extremely difficult to prove beyond reasonable doubt. What the courts have said—both in the Baltic countries and internationally—is that intent can be inferred from the specifics of the crimes themselves.

The cases against Soviet genocidaires in the Baltic countries have also concluded that exterminating part of a group can be viewed as genocide when the attack places the existence of the entire group in jeopardy. These rulings refer back in particular to the Srebrenica case, where the international courts decided in landmark rulings that the murder of nearly eight thousand Bosnian Muslims by Bosnian Serb military units was genocide because it was an attack on the entire people, using the crucial modifier of the genocide convention, "as such." In this legal context, one could conclude in retrospect that Stalin's assaults on many peoples in the course of the 1930s and early 1940s constituted an attempt to eliminate them "as such." The Ukrainian killer famine and the deportation and murder of Poles in the Soviet Union certainly fit this current of legal thinking.

Finally, the Baltic cases shed light in interesting ways on the question of whether genocide has to be carried out only against "other" ethnic, national, racial, or religious groups, as designated in the genocide convention, versus social and political ones. Since regaining their independence, the Latvians, Lithuanians, and Estonians have tended to ignore the unpleasant historical reality that native communists and local Baltic NKVD officers were sometimes directly responsible for the deportations, dekulakization, and the murderous attacks on the "forest brethren" and their supporters in the region. But the courts certainly understand this fact, since many of the defendants who have stood trial are Balts themselves and not Slavs. Does this make these attacks on the Baltic nations any less genocidal than if they were carried out solely by Russians or Ukrainians?

In perhaps the most celebrated case in the Baltic states, Arnold Meri, a cousin of the esteemed first president of Estonia, Lennart Meri, was put on trial in May 2008 for genocide in connection with the forced deportation of some 251 Estonians from the island of Hiiumaa to Siberia in March 1949. Forty-three of the deportees died in exile. Meri, who was the first Estonian to win the medal of Hero of the Soviet Union in World War II, pleaded innocent to the charges, insisting he was simply carrying out orders. Meri died in March 2009, before the trial concluded; the Russian president Dmitri Medvedev posthumously awarded him a medal for his service during the war.

It is important to note that the rhetoric of the campaigns carried out against the Baltic peoples by Moscow at the time was not directed against the particular nationalities themselves but against "bandits," "counterrevolutionaries," "kulaks," and "enemies of the people," similar to the rhetoric of Stalinist campaigns in the 1930s. The cases in the Baltic countries reflect a broader acceptance in international jurisprudence of political groups as legitimate victims of genocide, even if the 1948 convention implicitly excluded them from consideration. At the same time, in Argentina, a number of generals and high-ranking police officials were tried for genocide in connection with crimes of mass killing committed against their own "nation" in the period 1976 to 1983.[25] With this said, the Baltic cases also demonstrate that sometimes what appears to be a class genocide can have strong ethnic or national elements. In his important work on the Cambodian genocide, Ben Kiernan has demonstrated that social and ethnic criteria are not so easily separated from each other and often mix. From his research it is apparent that one cannot distinguish the Cambodian events from the normal patterns of genocide by using terms such as "autogenocide" or "social genocide"—there were too simply many ethnic components involved in the killing.[26]

We could say the same about Soviet attacks on Poles, Germans, Koreans, Ukrainians, and the peoples of the northern Caucasus, where—ostensibly—these actions were not, as best we know, initially intended to crush these peoples' collective identity as nations but in fact ended up attempting to do pretty much just that. The obverse is also true, as mentioned earlier. "Kulaks" became a "people," as did, in some fashion, "asocials" and the "Bloc of Rights

and Trotskyites." Their families were drawn into the vor-
tex of execution, exile, and death; their alleged social and
historical afflictions were to some extent or another seen
as inheritable. They were to be cleansed from society as
alien "elements" or "contingents." Political and social
groups became "imagined nations." The argument about
whether the Ukrainian killer famine was directed against
peasants or Ukrainians in this sense misses the point that
these categories blended so easily with each other. At the
very least, Stalin was determined to destroy their culture
and traditional way of life.

By any objective understanding of international law,
then, the kinds of attacks that Stalin's regime perpetrated
against the Soviet people might well have been included in
the genocide convention. That those kinds of murderous
Stalinist initiatives involving substantial social and political groups were not included in the convention against
genocide for essentially political reasons provides little
justification for scholars to exclude these crimes from their
definitions.

2 THE MAKING OF A GENOCIDAIRE

No serious observer doubts any more that Stalin was a cruel and brutal figure, one who supervised the deaths of millions of Soviet citizens without the least hesitation or self-doubt. Given the publication of relatively systematic research on the 1930s over the past fifteen years, there can also no longer be any question that Stalin was fully responsible for the mass killing during this period and knew the details of all of the major actions involved. We now have scores of declassified documents demonstrating that Stalin himself signed hundreds of arrest lists, checked off on the death sentences in most of them, constantly encouraged his underlings to carry out the "highest penalty" (death), and criticized others for misplaced softness and lack of vigilance against so-called enemies of the people. Dmitri Volkogonov relates a revealing story about Stalin reviewing an arrest (and death) list: "Stalin muttered to no one in particular: 'Who's going to remember all this riff-raff in ten or twenty years time? No one. . . . Who remembers the names now of the boyars Ivan the Terrible got rid of? No one. . . . The people had to know he was getting rid of all his enemies. In the end, they all got what they deserved'."[1]

Like a cat playing with mice, Stalin dangled the lethal prospects of deportation, life in the Gulag, torture, and execution in front of his subordinates, watching their reactions to his baiting, taunting, and sadistic humor. He sometimes set them up, supervised their arrests, gave them hope for reprieves, and then had them taken away to be interrogated, tortured, and shot. He even had the wives, children, and siblings of his closest confederates imprisoned or deported, while watching to see if they flinched or broke under the intense pressure. Neither Molotov nor Kaganovich did. When Stalin's comrades episodically committed suicide, sometimes leaving behind personal notes to him protesting their innocence, he was unmoved. Suicides simply proved that the accused were guilty, and in killing themselves they had tried to escape facing the just penalty for their crimes. Those who refused to confess were considered excessively proud and acting in defiance of the party. Those who confessed in order to save themselves and their families were simply executed or sent into exile because they admitted to their guilt. Their families were usually punished whether they confessed or not.

Stalin enjoyed the power of life and death that he held over a country of 170 million people (in 1938), and he exercised it without restraint. That he knew many of his victims personally only seemed to increase his jaundiced sense of play, even when the consequences were deadly serious. It was as if he was missing the frontal lobe of the brain in which empathy for his victims would have been found. There was absolutely no sense of regret at the number of the dead and broken, even when he called off the purges and killing or finally provided relief for the famines. Countless reports to him about the costs of forced deportation in the lives and welfare of Soviet citizens evoked no actions on his part and no expressions of remorse. The descriptions of the death agony of the Ukrainian killer famine of 1932–33, including widespread cannibalism, left him cold and unmoved.

The lives of Soviet citizens that were entrusted to his leadership were to Stalin—for all intents and purposes—without inherent value. Much is made of Stalin's later leadership during World War II, especially in today's Russia. But too few Russians ask the question how many of the twenty-seven million Soviet victims of the war could be attributed to Stalin's indifference to their loss, his readiness to place them in the line of fire without adequate weapons or protection, his continued willingness during the war to sentence hundreds of thousands of Soviet citizens to exile and potential death in the Gulag, and his countless mistakes as "generalissimo" and commander-in-chief.

Even after the war and the securing of Soviet status as a great power, the repressions and political murders continued, though on a reduced scale. His personal vainglory only became more pronounced with the victory over Nazism, while his xenophobia was fed by the outbreak of the Cold War. In late 1948 Stalin initiated a campaign against Soviet Jews as "cosmopolitans," spies for the Central Intelligence Agency (CIA) and agents of the "Joint" (the Joint

Distribution Service, a Jewish philanthropic organization). In June 1952 Stalin's security agencies concocted a conspiracy of mostly Jewish Kremlin doctors, the so-called Doctors' Plot, which may well have ended in the deportation to Siberia and the Far North of the Soviet Union's entire Jewish population. We still do not have convincing documentation on the plan to deport the Jews. Nevertheless, one can conclude with certainty that it was most fortunate for the Jews of the Soviet Union that Stalin died in March 1953, before any mass deportation action could have been implemented.

How does one account for the making of a mass murderer like Stalin? Was he born to kill? Or did the circumstances of his childhood and youth in the mountains of Georgia turn him into the brutal dictator who took so many millions of innocent lives? How does one factor in the influence of the Bolshevik faction of the Russian Social Democratic Party, a small and highly disciplined elite group of professional revolutionaries, which Stalin joined as a young radical? The Bolsheviks were led by Vladimir Il'ich Lenin, himself a figure ready to sacrifice innocent lives for the greater cause of making the revolution and securing its gains. Stalin genuinely thought that Lenin was the "mountain eagle" of the revolutionary movement and learned at his feet. During the Civil War Lenin advocated applying "the most draconian measures" to fight the counterrevolution and personally signed execution lists of hundreds of alleged members of the White forces.[2] Can we attribute Stalin's brutality to being the "best student of Lenin," as he was so often portrayed in Stalinist cant?

Further, one might ask whether the circumstances of
Stalin's seizure of power in the 1920s, which required
craftiness, guile, and conspiracy, fed the blood lust of the
victor against those whose political fortunes fell before
him. From being the supposed "errand boy" of the revolution and a problematic leader during the Civil War, Stalin
was elevated to become general secretary of the Central
Committee of the party and one of the major contestants
to replace Lenin. Stalin was not a political leader to toler-
ate resistance in any form, real, potential, or imagined.
Instead, he crushed his enemies, drove them into exile,
and had them killed. The actual circumstances of assert-
ing power against his rivals no doubt contributed to the
killing carried out by the Soviet government under Stalin's leadership. The very smell of blood, which was in the
Kremlin air in the 1930s, might well have fed the growing
violence of Stalin's regime.

Some of his biographers suggest that the death of his
first wife, Ekaterina (Kato) Svanidze, in 1908, soon after
the birth of their son Iakov, and the suicide of his second
wife, Nadezhda Alliluyeva, in 1932 prompted Stalin to
cut off his feelings for fellow human beings. Others have
asserted that Alliluyeva's death and the assassination of
Stalin's close confederate Sergei Kirov in December 1934
were the crucial set of events that isolated him from his
comrades and intensified his cold cruelty. His daughter
Svetlana Alliluyeva wrote that after the assassination of
Kirov, "Maybe he never trusted people very much, but
after their deaths [her mother's and Kirov's] [he] stopped
trusting them at all."[23] But the evidence for his coldness

in face of human suffering is more cumulative than that; it includes aspects of his childhood and immersion in the revolutionary movement, as well as his performance in the Russian Civil War and the political struggles of the 1920s. Nevertheless, until the early 1930s, Stalin was still able to experience periods of filial warmth in his family life and genuine friendship in moments of relaxation.

In short, there is no single key to understanding Stalin's violence in the 1930s, but rather—as is so often the case in the history of genocide—a perfect storm of factors intersected that brought Stalin to engage in the mass murder of millions. There was his own violent personality and development as a young man and revolutionary; his attachment to Bolshevism and the "hard" approach of Lenin to the problem of seizing and maintaining power; the very nature of Soviet power and its transformative Utopian communist ideology in a backward and traditionalist country; and the circumstances of Stalin's victorious struggle for power and his maximalist ideological goals. But before everything else, there was the malevolent and murderous leader. As Martin Malia writes: "The personal paranoia and the individual sadism of Stalin the man must constitute the decisive element that made his reign seem, in Bukharin's metaphor, like the return of Genghis Khan."[4]

Stalin was born Iosif Djugashvili in the Georgian mountain town of Gori, some fifty miles west of Tblisi (then Tiflis). This region of the Caucasus—beautiful and majestic—was also beset by poverty, economic backwardness, and Russian exploitation. The Georgians are a proud

and boisterous people who fostered their national identity
through traditional song, the Georgian Orthodox Church,
which predated Russian orthodoxy, and tales of bandits
and fighters, who defended Georgia's independence and
culture from the country's Iranian, Turkish, and Russian enemies. Most biographers give Stalin's birth date as
December 6, 1878, when Georgia was under the thumb
of the tsarist imperial administration and subjected to
Russianization campaigns directed from St. Petersburg
and carried out by local governors. As the son of Vissa-
rion (Besarion or Beso) Djugashvili, a young, handsome,
and rough-hewn shoemaker, and Ekaterina (Keke) Geladze, the intelligent, strong-willed, and pious daughter of
Georgian peasants, Stalin grew up amid both the poverty
and the religiosity of Georgian urban dwellers of peasant
background.

Some biographers would like to attribute Stalin's murderousness of the 1930s to the fact that his father was
known to have beaten him, sometimes quite brutally. In
fact, Beso grew increasingly fond of drink, and by the
time he finally abandoned his family in 1890, he had become something of an alcoholic. At the same time, Stalin's
mother was enormously devoted to her young son, especially given the fact that two other children had died in
infancy. But the picture of Stalin's youth is more complicated than that proffered by some of his biographers. His
mother was sometimes known to have beaten her son and
was very strict with him, while his father was probably not
untypical in using physical punishment against his son,
especially after having a lot to drink. In neither case does

the explanation of excessive physical abuse stand up to close scrutiny. Stalin himself mentioned to Emil Ludwig in an interview: "My parents were uneducated people, but they treated me not badly at all," and Svetlana Alliluyeva, Stalin's daughter, notes that her father told her: "Fights, crudeness were not a rare phenomenon in this poor, semi-literate family where the head of the family drank. The mother beat the little boy, the husband beat her. But the boy loved his mother and defended her: once he threw a knife at his father."[5]

In fact, young Stalin—Soso, as he was known to his family and friends—cannot be said to have had such an unusual upbringing for the Georgian urban lower-class milieu. He ran with his young friends in the streets of Gori and engaged in fisticuffs and unruly gang behavior, which were common at that time and place. He contracted a bad case of smallpox as a boy, leaving his face permanently scarred with unsightly pockmarks He also limped slightly from injuries sustained after being run over by one carriage and had a withered left shoulder and arm from being hit by another one. But it is also the case that at the religious school he attended in Gori, he was known as a very fine student and for having a beautiful singing voice. He read a lot and studied hard. Until very late in his life, he continued the habits of an autodidact that he picked up as a boy.[6] While some biographers portray young Stalin as a ruffian and thug, mean to animals and always ready for a fight, more characteristic of his youth was a proclivity to romanticism, traditional Georgian song, and poetry. This strong streak of romanticism deepened Soso's attachment to the Georgian national tradition and to the epic songs that were memorized by its youthful adherents.[7]

Like an entire generation of disaffected Georgian youth, Sosa recited the verses of Shota Rustaveli's *The Knight in Panther's Skin*, a twelfth-century epic poem that glorified Georgian national and heroic traits. One of Stalin's biographers writes that Stalin took some of his favorite sayings from Rustaveli, including: "My life is pitiless, like the beast," and "A close [friend] turned out to be an enemy more dangerous than a foe."[8] Among Stalin's favorite works were those of the Georgian patriotic writer A. Kazbegi, whose famous epic poem, *The Patricide*, extolled the virtues and heroism of Koba, the just avenger of the Georgian people. Koba, writes another recent biographer, "represented a noble ideal of a man of honor unwilling to submit to injustice."[9] Stalin clearly identified with Koba, adopting the name as his first underground pseudonym in 1903, and a few of his friends called him Koba until the end of his life. Even when he adopted the underground name of "Stalin"—man of steel, a perfect reflection of the image he wanted to project—shortly before World War I, for several years he would continue to use the letter "K" for Koba before Stalin.[10]

Stalin's mother was determined that her talented and beloved son should become a priest. For that purpose, she managed only with great determination and conviction to have him accepted as a scholarship student at the Georgian Orthodox Seminary in Tiflis. There, in 1894, young Sosa was forced to study Russian subjects in the Russian language under mostly Russian priests, which grated on

him and his classmates. Tiflis was the great multinational
center of the western Caucasus. Unlike the provincial
backwater of Gori, Tiflis exposed Sosa to the development of political radicalism in the Russian Empire, and
the emergence of the working-class movement. It was at
the seminary that Soso first read the radical literature that
suffused student circles throughout the empire in this period. For the first time, Stalin was introduced to Spencer
and Chernyshevskii, Darwin and Marx. Especially crucial
for Soso was the potent mixture of Georgian radical literature with the arguments of the Marxists against the
populists. Even as the eventual fount of Marxist-Leninist
ideology in the Soviet Union and around the world, Stalin
never lost his attachment to the Georgian literary tradition he absorbed as a seminary student.

But soon, too, Stalin would fall in with serious radical
groups in the city, where he got involved as a propagan-
dist among workers. In 1899 Stalin left the seminary for
good to engage full time in social-democratic circles. With
the police on his tail, Stalin went underground, moving to
Batumi, where he actively organized strike activities. Like
many young, educated, and idealistic imperial subjects of
the "periphery" (Congress Poland, Georgia, Armenia, or
the Pale of Settlement), Stalin was attracted to the growing strength and militancy of the workers' movement and
its social-democratic leadership. Already, Stalin demonstrated a number of character traits as a young revolutionary that persisted throughout his adulthood: intolerance of
differing opinions; a penchant for making enemies; and a
sullen, private demeanor. Many memoirists from the time

mention his "wry," "slight," or "mocking" smile, as if he knew something they did not and would not reveal it. At the same time he was restrained, quiet, and focused. His long-time associate Lazar Kaganovich remembered: "Stalin was not at all as he is portrayed [today]. . . . I know Stalin from the first period of his work, when he was a modest person, very modest. He not only lived modestly, but he carried himself modestly with all of us."[11]

Between 1902, when he was arrested in Batumi, and the revolution of 1917, Stalin was pursued by the police, was arrested and exiled twice, and lived underground as a social-democratic agitator. For short periods of time he managed to find his way to Europe and St. Petersburg on party business. He spent an especially formative period in Baku from 1907 to 1910, where his exposure to the powerful multinational oil workers' movement in the city convinced him that open agitation could often be as effective as underground propaganda. Above all, he learned flexibility in his methods and a realistic take on revolutionary opportunities. Dealing with the powerful Baku trade union movement forced him into a number of tactical adjustments. This hard-nosed pragmatism characterized his politics almost until the very end of his life, when he succumbed to the self-absorbed hubris of his old age.

Stalin's attachment to Bolshevism and to the radicalism of Lenin came quickly and unambiguously. Everything about Lenin appealed to the young Georgian radical: Lenin's dedication to a party of professional revolutionaries and to an uncompromisingly revolutionary brand of Marxism; Lenin's polemical style and intraparty combativeness; and Lenin's willingness to countenance labor violence and even terrorism if they forwarded the cause of the party of Social Democrats. Lenin was the founding father of Bolshevism. Young Koba, putting aside all of the hyperbolic rhetoric of the later cult of Stalin, quickly fell into step with the faction's ideology and its revolutionary tactics. In the name of the party, Stalin engaged in a series of bank robberies and "expropriations," the most spectacular taking place in Tiflis in 1907. Stalin's biographers sometimes cite these robberies as a sign of his lawlessness and violence; more appropriately, they should be seen as an example of his dedication to the welfare of the party and his lack of interest in traditional morality, something he shared with a number of Bolsheviks and Socialist Revolutionaries.

It would be wrong to think of Stalin as nothing more than a violent and conspiratorial Bolshevik, though he was certainly that. He was also an ideologist, and in his role as editor of *Pravda*, Stalin took on the important task of explaining the evolving platform of Lenin and the Bolshevik leadership to their followers. Stalin was an excellent editor, and he only got better over time. Though his Russian was not perfect, Stalin had a good understanding of the importance of punchy, agitational prose, and he was not averse to rewriting his comrades' contributions in that spirit. This was a talent he nurtured and exhibited until the very end of his life.[12]

Like many radicals of his day, Stalin spent time in tsarist exile for his revolutionary activities. His first experience of exile—1903–04 in the northern Irkutsk region—

proved to be relatively benign. He was able to read and write, to meet with fellow revolutionaries, and to develop friendships among the exiles. The same could be said of his exile to the Vologda region from 1909 to 1912. Especially compared to the conditions of those deported in the Soviet 1930s, Stalin's initial terms in exile seem downright luxurious. More difficult and serious for the development of his character was his exile in Kureika (in the Turukhansk region), north of the Arctic Circle, from 1914 until shortly before the revolution. Here Stalin lived in the extremely harsh and frigid circumstances of a tiny, isolated settlement. Less hardened men would have suffered terribly from the cold, the loneliness, and the company of the small native population. Stalin seemed to thrive, or at least to master his environment, finding comfort with local families (and women), and enjoying the solitude of hunting and fishing in the Far North. He emerged from this harsh environment even more controlled and sure of his ability to survive than earlier. When he joined the revolutionary upheaval in Petrograd in the early spring 1917, Stalin was a hardened and focused Bolshevik leader, capable of working long hours and carrying out designated tasks—and those he initiated himself—with efficiency and determination.

Stalin's role in the Great October Revolution was generally that of a follower and not a leader. Yet he was always there near Lenin, ready to take on the tasks that were assigned to him. On the one hand, he was Lenin's factotum; on the other, he made himself indispensable to many of his comrades by successfully accomplishing logistical and political assignments without complaint or hesitation. With so many self-important intellectuals involved in the revolution—Lenin, Trotsky, Zinoviev, and Bukharin among them—Stalin was content to be a party leader who spoke little but got things accomplished. It would be a mistake to think about Stalin as no more than a thug and messenger boy, an image that Trotsky successfully but misleadingly imparted to posterity. Stalin made things happen and created the circumstances in which he was destined to succeed.

During the Russian Civil War, 1918–21, Stalin served for a time on the Volga as the Bolshevik chief of the Tsaritsyn front. The Red effort in Tsaritsyn had been in chaos and was threatened with collapse when Lenin sent Stalin to shore up its defenses. On setting about his tasks, Stalin wrote to Lenin: "I harry and abuse all those who deserve it, and hope for early improvements. Be sure, we will spare no one, neither ourselves nor others." In response to Lenin's worries about the reliability of the Left Socialist Revolutionaries in Tsaritsyn, Stalin stated: "As for the hysterical maniacs, be sure that our hand shall not falter; with enemies we shall act as enemies." Stalin worked closely with the Cheka to bring order to the Red effort and to crush potential political opponents. Klement Voroshilov, who commanded the military in Tsaritsyn, described one typical case where "Stalin's decision was brief: 'Shoot!' The engineer Alexeyev, his two sons, and several officers with them, some belonging to the [alleged oppositional] organization, others only suspected, were seized by the Cheka and immediately shot without trial."[13]

The Civil War in Tsaritsyn proved to be a defining moment in Stalin's growing rivalry with Trotsky, who was commander of the Red Army. Stalin was incensed by the use of former imperial army generals and specialists in the army; he was convinced that they impeded the progress of the Red forces and undermined the cause of the Bolsheviks. Trotsky, on the other hand, thought it was necessary to employ this military talent in the struggle against the Whites. Meanwhile, Trotsky was openly skeptical of the crude Georgian's leadership abilities and was very critical of Stalin's inexperience and bungling in military affairs. The two denounced each other to Lenin and agitated for primacy in decisions on the Tsaritsyn front.

Despite Trotsky's allegations, Stalin proved capable of organizing the Reds' resistance to the Whites and of successfully carrying out the fundamental task of securing territory. Here, for the first time, Stalin experienced mass bloodletting, including summary executions and violent reprisals. To say he was responsible for the Bolsheviks' violence on the Volga front would be an exaggeration. But it is also clear that he did not shy away from taking the most extreme measures to secure Soviet power. In this, however, he was no less violent than Lenin himself, who was known to call for the demonstrative hanging of hundreds of peasants from hilltops ("hang without fail, *so the people* see"), as a way to quell uprisings, and to shoot supposed White opponents on the spot.[14] In any case, as Jörg Baberowski, among others, has argued, "In the excesses of the Civil War, Stalinism was brought to the world."[15]

Stalin also participated as a front commander in the Polish–Soviet War in 1920–21. Once again, questions were raised among the Bolshevik leaders about his lack of military prowess. Eventually, he was criticized—not surprisingly, especially by Trotsky—for having refused to sign on for the Warsaw offensive in favor of his own attack on Lwów. But the fact that the Poles successfully resisted the Red Army and were able to gain a favorable peace at Riga that guaranteed them advantageous borders to the east was not due just to Stalin's failings. The Soviet defeat in this war was not lost on Stalin—it seemed no defeat was: he had a long memory in this connection. His animus toward the Poles reappeared in vicious ways in the years to come. And, of course, his rivalry with Trotsky was further intensified; already by this point, writes Robert Service, "he was biding his time to take his revenge."[16]

Hard, cold, cruel, and impassive, Stalin experienced the victory of the revolution over its enemies and the establishment of Soviet power not as a source of joy and comfort, but as a challenge to his position within the Soviet hierarchy. His lust for personal influence, buried beneath a veneer of accommodation and compromise, meant that he would seek to inherit the position of Lenin in the party, when the Bolshevik paragon was felled by a series of strokes, the first in May 1922, and eventually died in January 1924. Of all the leading Bolsheviks, Stalin seemed to work most closely with Lenin. Their views on the New Economic Policy and the national question were also closer than often asserted in the literature.[17] It was therefore not unrealistic of Stalin to expect to lead the party after Lenin's death.

In his "Testament" (December 23–26, 1922), Lenin famously reviewed the positive and negative characteristics of a number of Bolshevik leaders, including Stalin, without indicating decisively who should succeed himself. However Lenin's addendum to the Testament, January 4, 1923, written under the influence of Stalin's bullying of the leaders of the Georgian party, made it apparent that the sick and dying Bolshevik leader worried about Stalin's personal characteristics, his "rude" behavior and harsh dealings with the comrades. That Lenin's wife, Nadezhda Krupskaia, soon thereafter complained to her husband that Stalin was mean to her and kept her from seeing him only increased Lenin's suspicions of Stalin's ambitions. But it was too late; Lenin died on January 21, 1924. Stalin's machinations surrounding Lenin's death and funeral, and his ability to portray himself as Lenin's most loyal pupil, demonstrated to those around him, especially his ostensible allies Zinoviev and Kamenev, that he sought supreme power. Lenin's Testament, with the addendum, was read to the Central Committee only much later, in July 1926, after Stalin, Zinoviev, and Kamenev had more or less secured control of the party leadership and could write off Lenin's remarks as the crotchety asides of an old and sick man.

The struggle for power in the mid- and late 1920s has been so thoroughly documented in the literature that there is no need to review it here. The charismatic and brilliant Lev Davidovich Trotsky, whom many believed would succeed Lenin as head of the party, increasingly isolated himself from the mainstream party leaders. His self-assurance, bordering on arrogance; his lack of attention to the party apparatus, something Stalin could never be accused of; and his frequent absences from the capital tarnished his reputation as a great leader of the Red Army during the Civil War and led many to doubt his ability to lead the Soviet state. The other major contestants for power, Zinoviev, Kamenev, and Bukharin, sought leading roles in the party and, like Stalin, wrote treatises on Leninism as a way to stake their claims. In the end, they all relied on Stalin to secure the party apparatus and deal with the mid-level party cadres.[18]

Stalin's ability to ally on the "left" with Zinoviev and Kamenev against Trotsky and then again with Rykov, Tomsky, and Bukharin on the "right" against Zinoviev and Kamenev, all the while appearing as a supremely disinterested advocate of party unity, guaranteed his success in this struggle. At the same time, Stalin fostered the careers of a series of stolid and capable subordinates, among them Molotov, Kaganovich, Mikoyan, and Voroshilov, who would support his attacks against Rykov, Tomsky, and Bukharin at the end of the 1920s. The methods developed by Stalin in the struggle for power served him well a few years later, as he organized the judicial murders of his political rivals, all "Old Bolsheviks," and instigated the genocidal campaigns that characterized the 1930s. He took his time to eliminate his rivals, and he plotted silently and well. "My greatest pleasure," he is known to have admitted, "is to choose one's victim, prepare one's plans minutely, slake an implacable vengeance, and then go to bed. There's nothing sweeter in the world."[19]

One learns a lot about Stalin's methods from reading the recently declassified internal debates of the Politburo and Central Committee plenums in the late 1920s and early 1930s, the crucial period for Stalin's "seizure of power."[20] These debates are fiercely polemical, with no holds barred. Yet Stalin remains aloof from the worst of the recriminations and poses as the arbiter of party unity. His is a voice of relative restraint, while others slug it out. Molotov, in particular, serves as Stalin's attack dog. Initially, Trotsky is the scapegoat, constantly on the defensive, yet also speaking too often and too aggressively himself. Once Trotsky is effectively removed from the scene in 1927, the "Right Opposition," Rykov, Tomsky, and, a bit later, Bukharin, become the lightning rods for failed policies and party intrigues surrounding the "Second Revolution," collectivization and the First Five-Year Plan. All the while, Stalin continues his pose as the rock-solid defender of the revolution and its accomplishments, though periodically he does ask hard questions and make sarcastic remarks about those under attack. His interventions are laconic and terse, those of a judge rather than of the prosecutor. But he could also slug it out and attack his opponents with cynical vitriol if he felt it necessary.

Stalin's posture in these party wrangles was, like so much else in his public life, an assumed one. He was an emotional man, who seethed with anger and resentment against his rivals beneath his calm surface, and he took great pains to keep his emotions in check.[21] Yet in his pri-

vate letters and in conversations with his closest confederates he revealed how deeply he was riddled with downright hatred. In a letter to Molotov of September 1930,
he uses language about Bukharin that he generally would
rarely use in public, calling him a *"rotten defeatist"* and a
"pathetic opportunist." In the same letter, he advises Molotov: "If Rykov and Co. try to stick their noses in again,
beat them over the head. We have spared them enough. It
would be a crime to spare them now."[22]

While the struggle for supremacy in the party itself did
not immediately lead to violence, Stalin's methods were
those of a determined conspirator and a skilled dissimu-
lator. His ability to adopt many poses and personae, depending on the needs of the moment, were characteristic of
his career to the very end. At the same time, his Georgian
habits, tastes, and personal characteristics never completely left him. After all, he wrote exclusively in Georgian
until he was twenty-eight years old.[23]

Who was Comrade Stalin? Very few really knew the
answer to that question, even when they thought they did.
Stories abound about Stalin's evasiveness when it came to
his person. Later in his life he would point to stylized, im-
posing portraits of himself and tell his interlocutors that
the image in the picture frame was Stalin, not the small,
unimpressive figure with sallow skin and a pockmarked
face that stood before them. When the actor Aleksei Dikii
was cast as Stalin in a movie, Stalin asked him how he
planned to play the role. The actor answered, "As the people see him." Stalin supposedly said "Right answer" and
gave him a bottle of brandy.[24] At the height of his power,

Stalin reportedly once yelled at his son Vasilii about exploiting his father's surname: "You're not Stalin and I'm not Stalin! Stalin is Soviet power!"[25]

The real Stalin—suspicious, vindictive, capable, cold, brutal, angry, self-possessed, and small, both physically and morally—eventually created the image of the imperial and grand Stalin. He lived within the magnanimous version of himself, while convincing those around him that it was real. By bullying, force, and manipulation, he attained enormous powers. Those who doubted or resisted the alchemy of Stalin's power and vainglory were demoted, stripped of their party credentials, and shunted off to the side. By the end of the 1930s they were sent to labor camps or shot.

3 DEKULAKIZATION

The Achilles heel of Soviet power, the problem to which the Bolsheviks returned repeatedly with little success, was the relative backwardness of the peasantry, which comprised the vast majority of the population of the Soviet Union. Everything about the peasants irritated the Bolsheviks: their religiosity and their attachment to customary law, their supposed primitiveness and inherently petit-bourgeois mentality. Throughout the late nineteenth century, European Marxists spoke of "the idiocy of rural life," full of the prejudices of urban elites and beliefs in the progressive qualities of the factory proletariat. Lenin at least understood that the Russian peasantry had some revolutionary qualities, and that poor and middle peasants could serve as the allies of the working class in a revolutionary situation. Indeed, in the revolution of 1917 the Russian peasantry served as an important combustible force—in the army as raw recruits, in the factories as newly recruited peasant-workers, and in the villages as landless and land-hungry farmers—that helped bring down the autocracy in February 1917 and chased the Provisional Government from power in October.

Many historians note that peasants are often the first to rise in revolution and the first to suffer at its hands, and the revolution of 1917 was no exception. True, the Bolsheviks' "Decree on Land" of November 8, 1917, granted the peasants' demand for ownership of the land, fulfilling the dreams of rural Russia since the peasant uprisings of the seventeenth century. But already in 1918, as the Bolsheviks desperately needed to collect grain for securing their power and fighting the Civil War, the peasants' rights to the land were quickly rescinded, and forced grain collection by armed groups of Red Army soldiers and hastily armed workers' detachments alienated the same peasant producers who had helped to bring down the old order with their violent rebelliousness (*buntarstvo*).

The Civil War in the countryside was brutal and lethal. Millions of peasants died in the conflict, some fighting on one side or the other, many simply caught in between the back and forth of the competing White and Red armies, Anarchists, Ukrainian factions, Cossacks, and the plethora of nationalist fighters. The forced expropriation of grain and attempts to collectivize the countryside led to pitched battles between peasants and the new representatives of Soviet power. Peasant uprisings broke out in the Tambov region and along the Volga. A terrible famine raged in the same regions and across Russia and Ukraine, as the policies of the Soviet government destroyed the productive capabilities of rural Russia. Lenin and the Bolsheviks had no choice but to exercise a retreat in the countryside, a so-called peasant Brest, a temporary compromise with the economic realities of the Soviet countryside. In 1921 the Bolsheviks introduced what was called the New Economic Policy, which called for a halt to forced grain requisitioning, allowed the peasants to accumulate and trade in grain products, and trumpeted the *smychka*, the alliance between workers and peasants. Many historians consider this simply a pause between the first major Bolshevik war against the peasantry (1919–22) and the second and final one to follow (1928–33).[1]

Certainly the NEP had economic and political costs that were unacceptable to Stalin and his allies in the Politburo. What is often called the "Second Revolution" in studies of the Soviet Union was really the breakneck and widely violent attempt by Stalin to steer the economy in a different direction and to save the Bolshevik Revolution—and his leadership of it—from what he feared was its potential disintegration. Therefore, in 1928 he introduced the First Five-Year Plan, which was intended to rapidly industrialize the country by pursuing improbably high growth rates. According to Soviet economists of the period, industrialization could be financed by "forced savings," meaning that the peasants would be required to sell their grain at low prices, paying higher prices for necessary industrial goods and consuming much less of their own production. The state would procure the grain and sell it abroad for the purposes of investing in industry.

Stalin regularly used the genuine fear of war and foreign invasion as the justification for his extraordinary measures in both industry and agriculture during the Second Revolution. "We have fallen fifty to one hundred years behind the developed countries," he lamented in a speech to leading industrial workers in February 1931. "We must make up this distance in ten years. If we fail we will be crushed."[2] Of course, Marxist-Leninist-Stalinist ideology predicted war and intervention: capitalism and imperialism would inevitably strike at the socialist usurper. Therefore the Soviet Union was to be placed on a constant war footing. But under Stalin, the war craze reached a new height, in part because of his own xenophobia and belief in the threats of invasion and in part because it provided a marvelously handy justification for ignoring common sense in economic matters and eliminating alleged political enemies, including the kulaks. During the Central Committee plenum in November 1929, at the outset of the collectivization campaign, Molotov returned to the theme of imminent foreign invasion as the motivation for Soviet policies. "We still have November, December, January, February, and March, four and a half months in which, if the imperialists attack us head-on, we can make a decisive breakthrough in the economy and collectivization."[3]

Given the peasants' unwillingness to part with their agricultural goods at lower prices—they would rather consume what they had or destroy it—Stalin embarked in 1929 on an accelerated program to collectivize the countryside. In the first two months of 1930, half of the Soviet peasantry, some sixty million people in over 100,000 villages, was forced into the hastily assembled collective farms.[4] No one should be mistaken about the essentially political goal of this program: to break the back of the independent peasantry. Never again would the "accursed peasants" be allowed to blackmail Soviet policy by withholding grain from the market. But through collectivization, Stalin would also implement the Bolshevik vision of a Soviet socialist countryside that had animated party veterans since the time of the revolution.

The vicious attack on traditional peasant agriculture was accompanied by Stalin's complete break with Bukharin, Rykov, and Tomsky, who opposed such irresponsibly violent "economic" measures, and by the introduction of Stalin's dictatorship. But we also need to recognize that Stalin was not alone in his maniacal disdain for the Russian peasantry and advocacy of collectivized agriculture: many Bolsheviks were nervous about NEP and unwilling to compromise with the countryside. They harbored a deep disdain for the so-called Nepmen, small-scale traders and entrepreneurs, who emerged during this period, as well as for the peasants who were able to hire labor and develop markets for their agricultural production. Many members of the Central Committee and Politburo supported Stalin's policies and found his arguments compelling.

The primary means by which the countryside would be transformed into collective farms was a radical—one could maintain—genocidal attack on the so-called kulaks, the supposed rich farmers who impeded the socialization of the land and exploited the poor and middle peasants, forcing them to work for little gain and depriving them of the land. (Kulak means fist; these peasants ostensibly were tightfisted and cheap with their supposed stashes of money gained at the expense of poor and landless peasants.) Historians of the Soviet countryside have concluded that the images of a socially diverse Russian peasantry, riven by class struggle and economic inequality, does not at all fit the real picture of rural life. Instead, there was considerable solidarity among peasants, richer and poorer, especially when facing the incursions of urban communists. Nevertheless, the kulaks became an imagined social enemy, a group that in practice was often defined by owning a few head of cattle and oxen or having a tin roof over their huts, but also by real and alleged opposition to collectivization and to communism, and sometimes merely by their religiosity or adherence to Old Believer communities. "From the first days of the Civil War," wrote *Izvestiia* in February 1930, at the outset of the dekulakization campaign, "the kulak stood on the opposite side of the barricades from us." The image of the kulak was abolutely consistent in Soviet rhetoric, remembered the later Soviet dissident Piotr Grigorenko: "this was a bloodsucker, an oppressor, and parasite."[5]

Village priests and their families were included in the kulak category, as were many former landowners. Some villages were simply identified as kulak villages and destroyed in toto by deporting their entire populations, richer and poorer alike. Like the peasants whom Lenin wanted to hang on every hillock in the Tambov region as a warning to the others to cease their rebellions, the kulaks became an imagined class of opponents to be destroyed, so that the rest of the peasantry would at best take up cudgels against them in class hatred and, at worst, silently and obediently join the world of the collective farm.

On March 15, 1931, the OGPU (security police) issued a memorandum on the kulak problem, which stated that the goal of deporting the kulaks from all agricultural regions was "to totally cleanse [them] of kulaks." There were essentially two categories of kulaks to be dealt with: the most dangerous would be "immediately eliminated," while the second would be exiled, a simple formula for punishment of alleged "enemies of the people" that was to be repeated throughout the 1930s. Meanwhile, Soviet activists in the countryside repeated slogans: "We will exile the kulak by the thousands and when necessary—shoot the kulak breed." "We will make soap of kulaks." "Our class enemy must be wiped off the face of the earth."[6] These were no mere slogans; the violence perpetrated by the dekulakization gangs, which sometimes included criminals among the rural poor and landless, was horrific. "These people," noted one OGPU report, "drove the dekulakized naked in the streets, beat them, organized drinking-bouts in their houses, shot over their heads, forced them to dig their own graves, undressed women and searched them, stole valuables, money, etc."[7] Even if directed and monitored from the Kremlin, there was much more spontaneous violence involved in the dekulakization campaign than in the later highly focused police actions against national, "asocial," and political victims of Stalinism.[8] In any case, between late 1929 and 1932, some ten million kulaks were forced from their homes.[9]

The combination of dekulakization and collectivization wreaked havoc in the countryside, prompting what some historians have suggested was a second civil war, as peasants burned their crops, slaughtered their cattle, and attacked the teams of communists and OGPU detachments sent from the cities and provincial capitals to ensure that Stalin's policies were carried out. The talk of class war in the countryside quickly faded, as it became clear that this was really a war of the city against the village, communists against the peasantry as a whole. There were more than thirteen thousand "mass actions" by peasants in 1930 alone, involving more than three million people. Many thousands of peasants died in these pitched battles, as did loyal Stalinists and OGPU members. In 1930 the Soviet regime passed 20,201 death sentences in the villages for political crimes, ten times more than in 1929. Most were associated with quelling rebellions in the countryside and enforcing compliance with collectivization programs.[10]

There were several characteristics of the dekulakization campaigns that should lead us to think about their genocidal qualities. First, Stalin ordered the attack on the countryside and entrusted its realization to his immediate deputies, including Genrikh Yagoda, head of the OGPU. Stalin oversaw the operations, eagerly read reports of their successes and problems, and made it clear from the beginning that no resistance was to be tolerated and that the kulaks were "to be eliminated as a class": killed, displaced, deported, and scattered in special settlements throughout the Far North, Central Asia, and Siberia.

Second, kulaks were defined in terms of families, not as individuals. Thus not only the head of the household and his wife were considered kulaks, but all of their relatives, young and old. The peasants who were labeled kulaks were deported as families and, indeed, sometimes even shot as families. Children of kulaks carried the mark of Cain throughout their lives, whatever their eventual jobs or professions. Kulakdom—if you will—was hereditary. This was, wrote Solzhenitsyn, "the nub of the plan: the peasants' seed must perish together with the adults."[11]

Third, kulaks were subjected to the kind of dehumanization and stereotyping that was common for victims of genocide throughout the twentieth century. They were "enemies of the people," to be sure, but also "swine," "dogs," and "cockroaches"; they were "scum," "vermin," "filth," and "garbage," to be cleansed, crushed, and eliminated. Gorky described them as "half animals," while Soviet press and propaganda materials sometimes depicted them as apes.[12] Kulaks in this sense were dehumanized and racialized into beings inherently inferior to others—and they were treated as such.

Fourth, kulaks were eliminated in large numbers. In the process of collectivization, some thirty thousand kulaks were killed, most condemned to death by quickly appointed judicial troikas and shot on the spot. The lucky ones were beaten, abused, arrested, and then sent into exile, their homes burned to the ground. Large numbers of kulaks—estimates range around the two million mark—were forcibly deported to the Far North and Siberia. Most of these were sent to so-called special settlements, which were scattered over the harsh landscape and in theory provisioned by the OGPU to hold the huge number of deportees.

The special settlements were an important dimension of the Archipelago Gulag, so poignantly described by Alexander Solzhenitsyn. However, Solzhenitsyn had little information about the special settlements, which swallowed up countless Soviet citizens in the 1930s and could be as lethal for their inhabitants as the better-known labor camps such as Vorkuta, Kolyma, and other similarly forbidding and fearsome imitations of hell. On paper, writes Lynne Viola, the special settlements were "a penal Utopia for isolating and reforging social enemies." In fact, they "became little more than a shoddily constructed institution of forced labor."[13]

In January 1932 the OGPU estimated that close to 500,000 kulaks, roughly 30 percent of the total number of kulak deportees at that time, had already died in the camps or had run away.[14] Leaving the deadly labor camps of the Gulag penal system aside, there is a real problem in thinking about the issue of genocide when it comes to the special settlements. Ostensibly, these settlements were designed to remove the kulaks from society—and later national groups and so-called asocials ("socially harmful elements")—and put them to supposedly productive work clearing forests, building canals, and plowing hitherto virgin farmland. They would labor in mines and settle regions inhabited by native peoples who were deemed by Soviet administrators as unfit for disciplined work. There was even the mantra that the kulaks, engaged in productive labor, might become respectable Soviet citizens again, despite their inherently rapacious character.

At the same time, the reality of the special settlements, which did not change much over the course of the 1930s and early 1940s, was that very few of the minimal re-

quirements for existence, called for in the directives setting them up, were present on the ground. We know this
from the numerous reports of shocked OGPU doctors and
settlement administrators, who describe hunger, disease,
filth, privation, fierce cold, and inadequate shelter and
food in virtually all of the special settlements. The timber
for building barracks never appeared; the machinery for
clearing land was absent; food rations, minimal to begin
with, were misdirected, stolen, or never sent in the first
place. The January 1932 report of one frustrated and
angry lower-level official in western Siberia by the name
of Shpek tells a familiar story about the general indifference to the suffering of the exiles.

> I was made responsible for setting up this camp. I
> set out in search of clothing and footwear for these
> elements, who lacked everything. I made the rounds
> of all the economic organs, obtained the necessary
> information, and then went to the District Com-
> mittee of the Party to inform Comrade Perepelitsin.
> Furious, he told me: "Comrade Shpek, you don't
> understand anything about the policies of our gov-
> ernment! Do you really think that these elements
> have been sent here to be reeducated? No, Comrade,
> we have to see to it that by spring they're all dead,
> even if we have to be clever about it: dress them in
> such a way that they'll at least cut down a little wood
> before they die. You can see for yourself in what con-
> dition they send them to us here, disembarking them

on the riverbank in rags, naked—if the government really want to reeducate them, it would clothe them without our help!"

... After this conversation, I refused to organize the camp, for I had understood that they were going to send people out there and that I was supposed to see to it that they all died.[15]

In his appropriately entitled *Cannibal Island*, Nicolas Werth describes the makeshift construction of one of these special settlements for contingents of so-called asocials or socially harmful elements. Transported from Tomsk to Nazino Island in the middle of the Ob River, some 6,600 to 6,800 people determined by the authorities to be "declasse" and "socially harmful" sought to stay alive in a frozen landscape without food, supplies, or decent shelter. The case was a particularly harsh one since the prisoners had no opportunity to escape, given the location, and no chance to seek help from neighboring settlements. Typically, the local authorities were completely unprepared to house and feed them. Barely 2,200 survived in these circumstances, but not before dozens of the exiles turned to cannibalism and necrophagy. Here and elsewhere in the Gulag and special settlements, the process of "decivilization" was noteworthy. Men and women were turned into animals by the Soviet state, represented by its warders, police, and settlement administration, but with full cognizance of its chief administrators in Moscow. This made it easier to shoot the prisoners—even hunt them as animals—and see them die. As was so often the case, the NKVD wrote a thorough report on the horrors of the Nazino camp's history, known to Stalin, and which Werth found more than seven decades later in the Russian archives.[16]

Certainly at the middle level of Soviet officialdom, conscientious observers understood that something was seriously wrong. Kulaks—including their families—were dying by the tens of thousands from hunger, typhus, and a variety of diseases induced by inhuman living standards and widespread famine. With their parents dead or dying, kulak orphans scavenged and begged throughout the Gulag system, looking for any way to stay alive. Cannibalism was rife and was widely reported by camp administrators and OGPU officials throughout the settlements and surrounding villages.

Stalin surely knew and understood that these conditions were ubiquitous and that the kulak population of the special settlements was being decimated month after month by the horrid conditions in which they lived. He was also responsible in many instances for reducing state funding for resettlement, which in turn made these conditions even more difficult for the kulaks to survive.[17] His indifference to this suffering and dying was certainly murderous, if not genocidal. Indeed, a good argument can be made that Stalin intended to wipe out the kulaks physically as a group of people—not just metaphorically as a class—and that therefore the result can be considered genocide.

The attack on the kulaks, not unlike the Turkish assault on the Armenians or the Nazi elimination of the Jews, came in waves. This first attack in 1929–30 was the most serious. After Stalin's article "Dizzy with Success," reported in *Pravda*, March 2, 1930, which with typical deviousness transferred blame for the excesses of collectivization from himself to overzealous local officials, the campaign was relaxed. But in the fall of 1930 and the beginning of 1931, the machinery for forcing peasants into the collective farms was again ramped up and few so-called kulaks were to remain in the countryside. These measures were complemented by draconian legislation against stealing state or collective property (August 1932), which made the theft of a small amount of grain or animal products punishable by death or exile. Especially during the onset of the famine years, this decree was discharged with particular frequency and harshness.

In typically cyclical fashion, the waves of attacks on the kulaks between 1929 and 1932 were followed by the relaxation of surveillance of the special settlements and the release of some kulaks from their terms of exile in 1932–33. Instead of returning to the countryside, hundreds of thousands of kulaks found their way out of the Gulag into major cities and industrial centers, where the severe shortage of industrial labor gave factory officials an incentive to ignore their background as "enemies of the people." In the deceptively calm political atmosphere of the mid-1930s, kulaks were able to establish themselves in jobs and positions around the country. Some were able to return again to their home villages and engage in agriculture. A few even made claims for the return of their property.

But this respite was only the lull before the storm. In connection with the election campaign to the Supreme

Soviet in December 1937, which was intended to ratify the new Soviet constitution of 1936, Stalin and his lieutenants were determined to eliminate any possible dissonance in the country during the highly publicized and well-attended speeches and electoral events. The constitution trumpeted the victory of socialism, the end of the class struggle, and the creation of the new Soviet man and woman. In this context, there was no room for the outliers of Soviet society—the so-called *lishentsy* (disenfranchised) and *byvshie* (former people). The police targeted especially kulaks and dekulakized peasants, but also vagrants of all sorts, prostitutes, ex-noblemen, ex-landowners, former tsarist officials, and the like. Once considered a "class" to be eliminated, the remaining ex-kulaks were lumped together with the "socially harmful elements," who were to be cut off from society and quarantined as a lethal danger to the state.

The campaign against these people who did not fit neatly into the Soviet social order had started already in the early 1930s, with the cleansing of "parasitic" elements, and was accelerated by the passportization campaign of 1932–33, which, at the same time, denied passports to peasants and to those urban dwellers who could not demonstrate their social usefulness to the regime. The passport became the way to distinguish between those who legitimately belonged to the accepted Soviet social world and those who did not and, moreover, threatened its integrity—at least in the distorted view of Stalin and the Soviet leadership—with their nefarious class views. The great Soviet Utopian project required social engineering of the sort that excised (their word!) millions of people from healthy society and transplanted them to areas of Siberia, the Far North, and Central Asia where they would be used as raw material for colonizing undeveloped territory. (The great imperial Russian historian Vasilii Kliuchevsky talked about the history of Russia as one of a country colonizing itself.) The only problem was that under the Soviet regime the colonists were deprived of their rights and often of their ability to survive.

This process of transforming the social composition of the Soviet socialist polity was entrusted to the NKVD, which was set up in 1934 to consolidate the police functions for the regime, including those of the OGPU. Campaigns for "social defense" were organized to rid the cities of supposedly harmful and marginal people. The NKVD routinely was able to suspend whatever civil rights that were available to Soviet citizens with the justification that the asocials, from the mid-1930s on known often as "socio-harmfuls" (*sotsvredniki*)—whether kulaks, indigents, vagrants, prostitutes, homeless, or others—were dangerous to state security. Those who experienced social problems and lived on the margins of society were conflated in the minds of Stalin and his police chiefs with counterrevolution writ large. In 1935 and 1936 alone, the authorities removed as many as 800,000 of these "harmful elements" from the most important Soviet cities and sent them off into exile.[18]

The cleansing of the cities had already begun in the 1920s and was accelerated in the early 1930s by the OGPU's grandiose plans to deport millions of people to colonize western Siberia and the North. Yagoda's successor, Nikolai Yezhov, sought with Stalin's connivance to complete this process by introducing the infamous Order 00447 in July 1937, which authorized the rounding up of any remaining "extraneous" outsiders in Soviet towns and cities and "socially harmful elements," meaning "former kulaks, criminals, and other anti-Soviet elements," and exiling them to the Gulag. The orders from the top included the setting of quotas for arrests in the various regions and the sending of NKVD and party officials to the provinces to ensure that the arrests and deportations were carried out without delay. According to the initial order, 268,950 people were to be arrested, of whom 75,950 were to be shot and 193,000 sent to camps. But as a consequence of a series of rolling orders (including Order 00485 involving Polish nationals and Order 00486, which authorized the arrest of wives of alleged counterrevolutionaries) the time frame for the campaign and the number of arrestees were both extended. The official final tally for Order 00447 was 767,397 tried by the troikas, of whom 386,798 were condemned to death and executed.[19] This is a shocking example of what Paul Gregory has called "Terror by Quota," a purposeful, planned, and murderous assault on "outsiders" in a society for no other reason than the perception that they were its potential enemies.[20]

Recent archival research has demonstrated the linkages between the promulgation of the new Soviet constitution in 1936, the election campaign to the Supreme Soviet in December 1937, and Order 00447 and its attack on "antisocial" elements and purported class enemies in the population. Since the constitution affirmed the voting rights of the entire adult population, the argument goes, Stalin and Soviet government officials worried that counterrevolutionaries would use the campaign and the secret ballot mandated by the constitution to undermine the Soviet state. Andrei Zhdanov, among others, claimed at the time that "our enemies are active and preparing concertedly for the elections." "The Constitution [of 1936] wasn't written for swindlers," stated the Moscow police to an "asocial" sentenced to eight years in the Gulag by an NKVD troika in November 1937.[21] In short, these newly enfranchised "elements" were either shot or sent off into exile before they had a chance to undermine the electoral campaign or vote.[22] The election campaign was also used to rouse suspicions of workers in the factories against their foremen, bosses, and party leaders. The process of "democratizing" the rank-and-file became, writes Wendy Goldman, "the means to a more thorough repression."[23]

Order 00447 spelled the end to any semblance of a normal life for those kulaks who had managed to evade arrest the first time around or those many tens of thousands who had tried to shed the black mark of their pasts by moving to the cities. Only during the Second World War were some kulaks, including youngsters who had never actually farmed the land, released from the special settlements and labor camps so that they could fight in the war. Also, from 1938 on, some kulak children under sixteen were allowed to leave the special settlements and shed their second-class status if they pursued higher education. There was still some commitment to the idea of "nurture" over "nature" in the Stalinist social engineering project.[24] Nevertheless, in the course of the 1930s Stalin and the repressive system he constructed and relied upon had quickly eliminated tens of thousands of kulaks and sent more than two million to the Gulag, where hundreds of thousands died in miserable conditions of hunger, disease, and extreme poverty. (In 1932–33 alone, 250,000 peasants died in exile.) Stalin set out to eliminate the kulaks as a class, and he did precisely that, by removing them from their land and sources of sustenance, to be sure, but also by sending them into the hell of the special settlements.

4 THE HOLODOMOR

The question of whether the Ukrainian famine of 1932–33 can be considered genocide has been a source of considerable historiographical contention ever since the publication of Robert Conquest's pathbreaking book, *Harvest of Sorrow*, in 1986.[1] We now know much more from published documents in Russia and Ukraine about the immediate causes and effects of the famine than we know about Stalin's motivations, which remain frustratingly elusive. There is also no consensus among historians about the numbers of victims, though the range of estimates, given access to the documents, has narrowed over the past fifteen years. Throughout the Soviet Union, the direct loss of life due to the famine and associated hunger and disease was likely to be six to eight million. Three to five million of this number died in Ukraine and in the heavily Ukrainian-populated northern Kuban, among the richest grain-producing areas in Europe.[2] The Ukrainian word Holodomor derives from a combination of the word for hunger *"holod"* and *"mor,"* to exterminate or eliminate.

The background to the Ukrainian famine of 1932–33 was economic and political, prompted by the Bolsheviks'

desire to modernize at unprecedented speed, as well as
the determination to break the back of the independent
peasantry throughout the USSR in the process. Stalin and
his immediate confederates began in 1928 a campaign of
forced industrialization, one that had been anticipated by
many in the Communist Party as a way out of the Soviet
Union's economic backwardness. The state would pay for
hyperaccelerated industrial growth by collectivizing the
peasantry and thus taking control of the grain harvest.
The only way to do this, the leadership insisted, was to
attack the kulaks, which meant violently removing the
supposed upper stratum of the peasantry from the countryside. This bloody and dysfunctional process, begun already in 1928–29, disrupted grain deliveries and made
the center more determined to requisition grain forcibly
from the peasants.

By 1931 the state collections of cereals in the largest wheat-growing regions of Ukraine and the northern
Caucasus constituted 45–46 percent of the entire harvest,
leaving the peasants bereft of food supplies.[3] Grain shortages led the peasants to slaughter their animals. Those
collective farms that still had supplies of seed grain for the
following year's harvest were forced to turn them over to
the authorities. There was nothing left to eat or to plant,
less because of the total size of the harvest (historians estimate that it was not so bad in 1932) than because of the
forced removal of peasant production.

Ukrainian peasants were resolutely opposed to Moscow's collectivization and grain-requisitioning policies. Almost half of all peasant uprisings against collectivization

in 1930 took place in Ukraine. But the Ukrainian peasantry was also "doubly suspect" to the center: as peasants, who were considered inherently counterrevolutionary and hopelessly backward by the Bolsheviks, and as Ukrainians, whose nationalism and attachment to their distinctiveness grated on Stalin and the Kremlin leadership. That the proponents of Ukrainian nationalism among the intelligentsia focused in their writings and speeches on the inherent characteristics of Ukrainian national culture that were preserved by the masses of Ukrainian peasants only increased Stalin's suspicions of rural Ukraine. Stalin harbored images of a fantastic plot in which the grain crisis would prompt Polish agents and Ukrainian nationalists to try to prize the republic loose from the union. "We may lose Ukraine," he ominously wrote to Kaganovich on August 11, 1932.[4]

Stalin insisted that grain should be collected from the Ukrainian peasants "at all costs," despite protests from local officials. On June 21, 1932, Stalin and Molotov, on behalf of the Central Committee, wrote to the Ukrainian party: "No manner of deviation—regarding either amounts or deadlines set for grain deliveries—can be permitted from the plan established for your region for collecting grain from collective and private farms or for delivering grain to state farms."[5] Widespread grain shortages in Ukraine due to the excesses of requisitioning led to fierce hunger and horrible desperation in the Ukrainian countryside, as well as in northern Kuban, heavily inhabited by Ukrainians. On November 27, 1932, Stalin ordered that a "knockout blow" be delivered to "some collective farmers and collective farms" that continued to resist requisition-ing. On February 19, 1933, he maintained that those who did not work—the so-called idlers—deserved to starve.[6]

The borders between Russia and Ukraine were sealed, and peasants were forbidden to travel by rail. Stalin was deeply angered that several tens of thousands of Ukrainian *kolkhozniki* (collective farmers) in search of food had "already fled across the entire European regions of the USSR and are demoralizing our collective farms with their complaints and whimpering."[7] In the month of February 1933 alone, cordons of OGPU troops arrested 220,000 Ukrainian peasants attempting to flee their villages. Of these, 190,000 were sent back home, which meant they were essentially condemned to death. The rest were sent to the Gulag, where the death rate during the famine years was also exceptionally high.[8]

Roadblocks set up by the authorities prevented Ukrainian peasants from entering the cities, where food was sometimes available, though far from plentiful. Even when the desperate peasants managed to elude the roadblocks and find their way to the city, they often collapsed and per-ished in the streets from lack of food. The authorities had the dead bodies quickly removed from sight. Offers of food relief to Ukraine from outside the Soviet Union were turned down as unnecessary; in fact, the Soviet authorities obsti-nately denied the very existence of the famine when they knew differently. This was very different from the terrible famine in 1921–22, when not only was the hunger of the peasantry widely acknowledged, but the famous American Relief Administration (ARA) mission, initiated by Herbert

Hoover and facilitated by Maxim Litvinov, was allowed to enter Russia and provide widespread help to sick and hungry peasants. By contrast, as the crisis worsened in the course of 1933, Stalin, Molotov, Kaganovich, and others in charge of dealing with requisitioning and punishing resistance increasingly tended to blame the Ukrainians for the famine (a shift from blaming the kulaks!).[9]

The death agony of the Ukrainian countryside was heard in the Kremlin, but neither Stalin nor anyone else in the leadership did anything about it. Nor did they seem to care. When the Soviet writer Mikhail Sholokhov wrote to Stalin in April 1933 to complain about the terrible effects of the famine on the Soviet countryside, which he had witnessed firsthand in the northern Caucasus, Stalin responded that the problems were caused by the peasants themselves. "The fact that this sabotage was silent and appeared to be quite peaceful (there was no bloodshed) changes nothing—these people deliberately tried to undermine the Soviet state. It is a fight to the death Comrade Sholokhov!"[10]

Can the Ukrainian famine be considered genocide? It would seem so. There is a great deal of evidence of government connivance in the circumstances that brought on the shortage of grain and bad harvests in the first place and made it impossible for Ukrainians to find food for their survival.[11] Most scholars agree that there was enough grain in the Soviet Union in this period to feed everyone in Ukraine at a minimal level. The state's strategic reserves were estimated at three million tons, enough to provide crucial relief for almost all of the starving peasants. But forced requisitioning removed the margin of sufficiency and sank the region into famine, desperation, and cannibalism.[12] The Soviet Union continued to export grain in substantial quantities (some 1.8 million tons in 1933) to meet its obligations abroad and fund industrialization.[13] There had been food riots and strikes in the cities during the spring of 1932; Stalin and his lieutenants decided that they would feed the cities and workers but not the Ukrainian class and national enemies in the countryside. Some scholars have noted that the Soviet authorities actually did come up with some famine relief for the Ukraine in "piecemeal Politburo decisions," and that grain exports were cut back substantially at the beginning of 1933.[14] But this relief was too little, too late; millions had already died, and thousands more deaths would follow. In the end, there may well have been two stages of the Ukrainian drama: the first in 1930–31, when the famine broke out and threatened wide areas of the country as a whole; and the second in 1932–33, when Ukrainians in particular— unlike Russians and Belorussians—were given no opportunity to seek or receive help.[15]

Complicating the analysis of the Ukrainian killer famine is the fact that many non-Ukrainian areas of the country also suffered from severe hunger and famine during this period, including Russian and Belorussian regions. In the tragic case of Kazakhstan, with its extensive nomadic and seminomadic agricultural base, the conditions of famine were even more severe than in Ukraine. The number of

deaths attributable to the famine was 1.45 million, some
38 percent of the total Kazakh population, the highest percentage death toll of any nationality in the Soviet Union.[16]
Here, Moscow's shameful neglect of the negative effects of
having destroyed the Kazakhs' nomadic economy with its
compulsory policy of "sedentarization" was the primary
cause of starvation, rather than any purposefully murderous action on the part of the government.[17] Kazakhs were
not prevented from escaping famine-struck regions or
seeking aid in the cities and towns, though there were serious efforts to keep them from fleeing across the sparsely
guarded border into China. Many Kazakhs were shot and
killed trying to flee the country. At the same time, neither
the Kazakhs nor the Ukrainians were provided relatively
quick and effective relief, that reached some Russian and
Belorussian areas struck by the famine.

Similarly, in neither Kazakhstan nor Ukraine did the
authorities, when confronted with the realities of a starving population, immediately relax the conditions of forced
requisitioning, as they did in some other regions struck by
famine. For these reasons and others, some scholars have
called the Kazakh famine genocidal, despite the paucity
of documentation regarding Moscow's intentions. Kurt
Jonassohn writes: "There is no doubt that the deliberate
starvation of the Kazakh people, coupled with the purges
of Kazakh intellectuals and cultural leaders, makes this
a clear case of genocide."[18] Given the fact that the apparent goals of Moscow's Ukrainian and Kazakh famine
policies were the same—to destroy particular ways of life
that were closely associated with the distinctive national

and ethnic cultures of the people involved—Jonassohn's conclusion makes some sense.

There is not a lot of evidence that Stalin himself ordered the Ukrainian killer famine, but there is every reason to believe he knew about it, understood what was happening, and was completely indifferent to the fate of the victims. This may not be enough evidence to convict him in an international court of justice as a genocidaire, but that does not mean the event itself cannot be judged as genocide. Recent international jurisprudence concludes that a historical event—such as the massacre in Srebrenica in July 1995—can constitute genocide without the demonstration that specific perpetrators were guilty of the crime. The Srebrenica massacre was also judged to be genocide because the aim was to attack the whole nation by destroying part of it, "as such," which also applies to the Ukrainian case. Slobodan Milošević died before his trial before the ICTY was concluded, but it is also unlikely that he would have been convicted of genocide, though—like Stalin and the Ukrainian famine—he was ultimately responsible for the Srebrenica events.

Paradoxically, part of the problem in labeling the Ukrainian famine as genocide derives from the generally brutal character of Kremlin policies carried out against the regime's own people. This harsh regime began already in the time of Lenin, though most historians agree that Stalin's crimes against the peoples of the Soviet Union reached an unusual, even pathological, level. If as many as twenty million Soviet citizens may have died at the hands of the regime during Stalin's rule, and millions of others languished in camps, prisons, and special settlements, then the Ukrainian famine becomes only a part of a larger framework of criminal, if not genocidal, actions carried out by Stalin and his ruling circle.

A further problem in analyzing the Ukrainian famine as a case of genocide is the complete indifference to human suffering that permeated the Soviet ruling circles in Stalin's time. If Ukrainian peasants starved to death in the hundreds of thousands, even millions, does the lack of any effort whatsoever to relieve their suffering indicate genocide? Probably not. But in the Ukrainian case, even more convincingly than in that of the Kazakhs, there are good reasons to believe that the famine itself was intensified, if not intentionally precipitated, by the same Stalinist leadership that not only refused to undertake any efforts to help, but did not allow the victims themselves to seek sustenance or escape. If Stalin and his ruling circle created these circumstances because they distrusted peasants and were indifferent to their suffering and dying during collectivization and dekulakization, then, in a strict sense, the 1948 definition of genocide does not apply to the case. If the victims were allowed to perish because they were Ukrainians, then the indictment of genocide under the 1948 definition makes perfect sense. Of course, Stalin did not want to kill all the Ukrainians or deport them all to Siberia, the Far North, and Central Asia. But he did want to destroy them as the enemy nation he perceived them to be and to transform them into a Soviet nation that would be completely reliable, trustworthy, and denationalized in all but superficial ways. The bottom line is that Stalin,

Molotov, Kaganovich and their ilk were convinced that the Ukrainian peasants as a group were "enemies of the people" who deserved to die. That was enough for the Soviet leadership; that should be enough to conclude that the Ukrainian famine was genocide.

5 REMOVING NATIONS

Stalin helped to forge Soviet nationality policy when he was Commissar of the Nationalities from 1917 to 1924. Already on the eve of the revolution, he had written his famous essay "On the National Question," which argued that national self-determination and regional autonomy should be part and parcel of the revolutionary program of the Bolsheviks in the periphery. During the 1920s he—along with other Bolsheviks—supported the policies of *korenizatsiia*, which essentially allowed, indeed encouraged a level of autonomy and particularistic cultural development to all national groups in the Soviet Union, no matter how big or small. There is good reason to believe that Stalin was less enthusiastic than others about the increasing willingness of national groups not only to express their cultural and linguistic differences and to make their own educational and economic policies, but to ask for formal independence. Stalin's role in the "Georgian Affair" (1923), in which he was known to have bossed around and abused Georgian communists, gave Lenin reason to think about Stalin, despite his Georgian background, as a Great Russian chauvinist.

Inevitably, the Bolsheviks would have to rescind their promises in the Decree on the Rights of the Peoples of Russia, November 15, 1917, which guaranteed not just autonomy but even the right of secession to nations that wanted it. But more shocking to communists among many of the nationalities was the backtracking on some aspects of *korenizatsiia* and the overall reassertion of control by Moscow and Russians over the national units that occurred in the early 1930s. The Ukrainian famine was just one piece—though an important piece—of a broader program to crush potential opposition among national groups, large and small. The Second Revolution included not just draconian measures to promote industrialization, collectivization, and dekulakization, as well as deft political machinations to ensure Stalin's dictatorship. It also decisively ended the dream of a true union of socialist republics, each with its own national character and autonomous government. Stalin transformed the Soviet government from one that fostered the development of the nationalities, indeed creating nationalities in the process, to one that treated them differentially according to Moscow's perception of their political reliability, while eliminating some of them in administrative and even genocidal actions.[1]

Like the attack on the kulaks, the assault on selected nationalities took place in waves, some more extreme in their scale and violence, some less so. The initial victims of these attacks were the peoples who could be considered diaspora populations of states beyond the borders of the Soviet Union: Germans, Poles, and Koreans. Under

Stalin, the regime began to draw sharp distinctions between "Soviet" nations and "foreign" nations, designating the latter as "unreliable elements."[2] Members of these nationalities were considered particularly dangerous in the 1930s with fears of an approaching war: the Soviet Germans were a potential fifth column for Nazi Germany; the Soviet Koreans would support Japanese imperialism in eastern Siberia, where they lived; and the Soviet Poles were instruments of the intrigues of Pilsudski's Poland against the Soviets. But it would miss the essence of the attacks on these peoples to exaggerate the real threats that they posed to Stalin and Soviet power. Not only were the number of spies among these peoples very limited, but there was no reason to think they would be any less loyal during a war than the Russians, Uzbeks, or Belorussians, who were not attacked at all in the same way.

The vulnerability of the Soviet borders is a matter of historical dispute. But one might suggest that in an environment in which railway accidents, shortfalls in mining production, and grain spoilage were routinely attributed to Trotskyite subversion and Japanese-German spies, resulting in tens of thousands of arrests, torture and forced confessions, and thousands of executions, the war scares and spy mania in the borderlands were part of the same process of inventing enemies and destroying people ultimately for no other reason except to maintain the suspicious and vengeful dictator in power. Of course, the dictator could not separate his own interests from those of the party and state, and highly exaggerated foreign threats became an essential part of both the rhetoric and content of Soviet policy making. As we have seen, the threat of war and invasion had been used to justify the First Five-Year Plan, collectivization, and dekulakization at the end of the 1920s and the beginning of the 1930s, even before Hitler had come to power and the Japanese had invaded Manchukuo. Moreover, the campaign against the nationalities was suspended precisely in 1938–39, when the war was indeed imminent! Much like Marxist-Leninist-Stalinist ideology itself, the threat of foreign invasion became an aspect of the lenses through which Stalin and his lieutenants viewed the world around them. It both justified and motivated their actions independent of the social reality faced by them or of the actual threat of war from abroad.

Certainly there were signs of the coming of European war on the continent, and Japanese aggression was a fact in East Asia at the end of the 1930s. The events of the Spanish Civil War (1936–1939) heightened Stalin's paranoia about subversion and hidden enemies. The Polish intelligence services did indeed send spies to infiltrate the borderlands and Soviet interior, as did the Japanese and the Third Reich. However, it was hardly the case, as Kaganovich asserted at the February 28, 1937, plenum of the Central Committee (in connection with the issue of the alleged "Japanization" of the Soviet railway system), that "Japanese-German-Trotskyite agents" had engaged in widespread "wrecking, diversion, spying" on the railways and that they were in cahoots with Soviet bureaucrats and workers at all levels of the state railway administration. It also made no sense that, as Stalin asserted, these spies were ready to jump at the throat of Soviet power once the war began.[3] It should come as no surprise that the railway administration was purged at every level, perhaps more than any other single state institution. The gutting of the railways and the marked increase in accidents in 1938 and 1939 made it something of a miracle that the Soviets were able to transport their industries in Ukraine to the east so rapidly after the initial German advances in June 1941.

In sum, the forced deportation and persecution of national groups resulted primarily not from the real threats of war and infiltration, but from Stalin's generalized xenophobia and his pathological fear of losing power through subversion, whether of the Fourth International or by hostile powers beyond his borders.

The first major actions against the nationalities took place in 1932–33, when the borderlands of the West were "cleansed"—the Soviets' word—of allegedly dangerous and traitorous Poles and Germans. Some 150,000 Polish and German families—meaning roughly 500,000 people—were arrested and deported to the special settlements, joining the kulaks and "asocials" who already inhabited large stretches of the same territory. The same terrible conditions existed, and many of the deported perished in exile. The Great Purges of 1937 and 1938 also hit the nationalities disproportionately hard. The "rate of extermination" (the percentage of death sentences) was significantly higher in cases against "national" versus social and political enemies.[4] As Old Bolsheviks and members of the *nomenklatura* were accused in the hundreds of thousands of being spies and agents of foreign powers, those foreigners who resided on Soviet territory were assumed to be in the pay of their respective "home" country's secret services: Germans of Nazi Germany, Poles of sanacja Poland, French of France, the British of Great Britain, and so on. Those Soviet citizens who had contacts with foreigners, worked for foreign firms, or had lived abroad were also immediately suspect and were often arrested, purged, and exiled. Many were shot.

The "German operation," for example, included German citizens in the USSR, Soviet citizens of German origin, former personnel of German companies of all backgrounds, political emigres, deserters, and so on. Many non-Germans who were associated with Germans in any way were also arrested in the operation. Some 65,000 to 68,000 people were arrested; 43,000 of them were condemned to death.[5]

While some Germans—those from the Volga German autonomous republic, for example—were not the subject of special "repressions," the Poles, in the words of one NKVD official, were to be "completely destroyed." Stalin was pleased with Yezhov's fierce campaign against the Poles. "Very good!" he wrote on Yezhov's report about its initial stages. "Dry up and purge this Polish espionage mud in the future as well. Destroy it in the interest of the USSR." This genocidal language complemented NKVD orders to arrest entire Polish families as well, sending the women to the Gulag and the children under fifteen to NKVD orphanages. In the end, some 144,000 people were arrested in the Polish operation, 111,000 of whom were shot. Whatever the real danger to the Soviet Union of

Poland and Polish spies, the NKVD imbibed Stalin's Polonophobia,[6] supporting the campaign against the Poles by distorting evidence from its own Soviet spies in Poland that indicated the danger was less than that trumpeted by the authorities and encouraging stereotypical images of the "Polish threat."[7]

Even foreign communists in the Soviet Union and in Europe were suspected of spying, wrecking, and treason. Those out of the reach of the NKVD were called home to Moscow and eventually arrested. Stalin completely disbanded the Polish communist party in 1938; its leaders were executed or exiled; and its members were sent to the Gulag as agents of the Warsaw government and simultaneously of Trotsky! The large number of Soviet Poles in the NKVD—many were originally recruited by the Polish Bolshevik and Cheka founder Feliks Dzerzhinskii—were also purged during this period. Many were shot as agents of the Polish government.

German communists faced a similar fate, though the party itself was kept intact. In February 1940 some 570 German communists were handed over to Stalin's Nazi allies in an exchange of prisoners at Brest-Litovsk. Many of those lost their lives in the gaols and concentration camps of the Third Reich. In all of the national operations, justified uniformly as efforts to deprive the enemy of a potential fifth column during a potential war, 350,000 people were arrested, 247,000 of them executed.[8]

The Great Terror marked a general transition in state repression from social to national groups. After 1937, for the first time in Soviet rhetoric, the "Great Russian nation" was elevated above the others. At the same time, the government disbanded as reactionary and unnecessary many smaller national units and subunits that had existed since the early 1920s as distinct administrative entities.[9] In the second half of the 1930s, Poles, Germans, Koreans, and Iranians who lived in border regions met the bitter fate of executions, forced deportations, and scratching out new lives in special settlements and the Gulag. On the eve of the war, Ukrainians, Finns, and Estonians were "cleansed" from their homelands en masse and in a similarly brutal fashion.

In 1937 the first "total" forced deportation of a people took place when Stalin ordered the resettlement of the Koreans, some 175,000 people altogether, from the Soviet Far East to Kazakhstan and Uzbekistan. The Koreans suffered extreme privations during this large-scale transfer. It took them more than a month to reach their destinations. Like the kulaks, they showed up at settlements that had none of the building materials, supplies, food, and heating materials that had been assured by government orders. Some four thousand Koreans who arrived in the town of Kustanai spent at least a week in their train cars before the local authorities did anything to help them.[10] The real threat of Japanese subversion of the Korean population was in no way proportionate to the harsh fate of the Koreans. In this case, Stalin struck at the Koreans for no other reason than that there was a Japanese threat in the East, not because the Japanese could and did use the Koreans, nor because there was evidence the threat of Korean collaboration would turn into an actuality at any time soon.

The Korean deportation was an important milestone in
the history of Soviet actions against the nationalities, even
though there were some notable exceptions to their generally harsh treatment.[11] Soviet officials learned lessons
about how to conduct military-like operations against their
own people, using surprise and speed as their most valuable weapons to uproot masses of unsuspecting citizens.
They developed techniques—if still imperfect—for trans-
porting at once large numbers of people by rail. NKVD
special units both at the point of embarkation in the Far
East and on arrival in Central Asia learned the business of
the mass deportation of an entire people, old and young,
workers and peasants, party members and not.

Stalin's campaign against foreign nationalities subsided
as the war appeared imminent. The Great Terror against
other categories of "enemies of the people" was also called
off when Beria replaced Yezhov as head of the NKVD in
November 1938 on the eve of the war. Beria then proceeded to purge the entire NKVD organization, much as
Yezhov had purged the Yagoda-led security police. With
deceptive innocence, Beria accused the NKVD's previous
leaders of allowing excesses against perfectly loyal Soviet
citizens, engaging in torture to extract false confessions,
and unjustly punishing family members.

As a consequence of the secret protocols of the Nazi–
Soviet Pact of August 23, 1939, whose existence Soviet
authorities denied until December 1989, the Soviet army
occupied Estonia, Latvia, Lithuania, eastern Poland
(western Belorussia and western Ukraine), and Bessarabia
(Moldova). During the period 1940–41 Soviet authorities

seized control of these territories and incorporated them into the Soviet Union, deporting hundreds of thousands of people in the process. Some scholars from the Baltic states today regard the deportations (6,000 Estonians, 17,000 Latvians, and 17,500 Lithuanians) as the first stage of genocide, especially when combined with murderous military actions against Baltic resistance fighters (the "forest brethren") resulting from the reconquest of these territories in 1944–45, and renewed deportations in association with collectivization and dekulakization in 1948–49.[12]

The total number of Baltic peoples deported to Siberia, Central Asia, and the Far North in this period was 118,599 from Lithuania, 52,541 from Latvia, and 32,540 from Estonia.[13] The majority of those deported in the initial period of the Nazi–Soviet Pact were members of the ruling elite and intelligentsia; in the period 1948–49 the majority of those sent off were alleged kulaks and middle-class townspeople. They were all told that the deportations were "forever," and many tens of thousands died in exile. In other words, the forced deportations of the Baltic peoples were not so much punishment for crimes against the Soviet state as they were part of the Soviet effort to refashion the Baltic social structure and absorb these countries into the Soviet polity.

During World War II Stalin and the Soviet government intensified the attacks against the Poles that had characterized the previous decade of repressions. Whereas in the 1930s Soviet Poles were the primary targets, during the war Polish citizens located in Soviet-occupied territories were arrested, deported, and sometimes executed by the Soviet authorities. But the language, the style, and form of the repressions were the same. In 1940–41 over 300,000 Poles, mostly women and children, were forcibly deported from their homes in Soviet-occupied eastern Poland (western Belorussia and western Ukraine) to special settlements in Central Asia, the Far North, and Siberia. Many thousands of women and children died in the pitiful circumstances of exile, even after a formal "amnesty" was proclaimed in the summer of 1941.[14] Many other Poles were seized and imprisoned, including approximately 22,000 army officers, as well as government officials, religious leaders, and professionals, most of whom were also reserve officers in the Polish army.

We now have the documents to fill in the details of what officials of the Polish Government-in-Exile suspected from the very beginning: that Stalin and Beria ordered the execution of these detainees with the justification that "they are all," in Beria's words, "sworn and incontrovertible enemies of the Soviet state" and would sooner or later cause trouble for the Soviet authorities. The cases would be "processed without summonses, statements of accusations, preliminary investigations, or bringing of charges." Instead, a Politburo resolution of March 5, 1940, approved the "maximum penalty: death by shooting"; and special NKVD troikas confirmed the predetermined outcome. [15]

In April 1940 the Polish officers and men, located at three major NKVD detention camps, Kozelsk (east of Smolensk), Ostashkov (near Kalinin/Tver), and Starobelsk (near Khar'kov), and several additional locations in western Ukraine and western Belorussia, were driven by trucks to isolated local forests and fields, executed with a shot in the back of the head, and buried in mass graves. Some were killed right away in various NKVD installations. A few escaped execution by convincing their NKVD interrogators that they would work for the Soviet cause. When the Nazis discovered the graves of 4,400 victims in the Katyn forest in the early spring of 1943 and tried to exploit the killing for anti-Soviet propaganda purposes, Stalin and his lieutenants were able to convince their Western allies that this was all a Nazi hoax. At Nuremberg and after, Soviet denial was a major source of justifiable Polish anger, frustration, and enmity toward the Soviet Union, to be sure, but also toward the Western Allies, who had refused to take up the cause of the murdered Poles, even when they began to suspect that the Soviets had murdered the officers.

What became known in subsequent accounts as the Katyn Forest massacre was a mirror action to the Nazi Operation Tannenberg, carried out in the first months of the German occupation of Poland. In that operation the SS had assembled lists of sixty thousand members of the Polish intelligentsia to be hunted down and executed. Hitler's idea was to decapitate the Polish nation by destroying its leadership: priests, schoolteachers, government officials, and military officers, among others. Deprived of its elite, the Polish nation would serve the Third Reich as workers, helots. Stalin's idea was pretty much the same: to destroy the ability of the Poles to resist the Soviet takeover of their eastern territory. Molotov could scarcely contain his glee at the signing of the Nazi–Soviet Pact and its consequences, when he stated in October 1939: "One swift blow to Poland, first by the German Army, and then by the Red Army, and nothing was left of this ugly offspring of the Versailles Treaty."[16]

There can be no question that Stalin and Beria ordered the mass executions of the 21,857 Polish officers and men for the purposes of mutilating the Polish nation. It also was the culmination of a decade of actions against Polish citizens of the Soviet Union and of Poland that were rationalized by the ostensible Polish threat to Soviet territorial integrity. There is good reason to think that these actions, when looked at as a whole, derived from deeply embedded Russian and Soviet prejudices of anti-Polonism—the Pole as nobleman (*"Pan"*), as the effete yet dangerous, inherently exploitative, and untrustworthy neighbor of the East Slavic peoples—Russians, Ukrainians, and Belorussians.

The Katyn act of mass murder in June 1940, denied by the Soviet regime until the very end of its existence and skimmed over by Western commentators during the war, at Nuremberg, and even after, should be considered one of the most unambiguous cases of genocide in the history of the twentieth century. On December 29, 1989, the Congress of People's Deputies publicly recognized the secret protocols for the first time in Soviet history and apologized for them. However, during the Putin era, especially, one hears very little about the Soviet depredations during that infamous period of occupation, forced deportation of peoples, and genocide. The Russian government has criticized recent commemorations of the seventieth anniversary of the Nazi–Soviet Pact for one-sidedly ignoring the

Soviet Union's difficult strategic situation in 1939 and unjustly criticizing its attempts to defend its Soviet territory.

Stalin's animus toward the Poles, Germans, and Koreans was matched by his growing mistrust of many non-Russian peoples inside the Soviet Union. These nations did not have "homelands" outside the USSR's borders to spy for, which might lead one to think that perhaps it was not the real threat of these or other peoples' treachery that motivated Stalin's actions against them. The mistrusted nations—the "punished peoples" in Alexander Nekrich's pioneering work—included, perhaps most importantly, the Ukrainians.[17] But the terrible mass starvation of the killer famine of 1932–33 could not be followed by a full-scale deportation to Siberia and the Far North; there were quite simply too many Ukrainians to deport them all, and too much fertile agricultural land in the Ukrainian steppe that needed able farmhands.

During the war Stalin focused his campaign against suspected traitorous nations on the Muslim peoples of the northern Caucasus and Black Sea littoral. There is no necessary reason to think that Stalin developed his suspicions about these nations as a consequence of his Georgian background, though this may well have played a role. Much more salient was his mistrust of the independence and stalwart opposition of Chechens and Ingush (related northern Caucasus peoples), Balkars, Karachaevtsy, Crimean Tatars, and others to collectivization and to the general regimentation of political, cultural, and social life emanating from Moscow. Archival materials from the 1930s show that even Chechen party leaders refused to allow their wives to be engaged in the economy, and that Chechen mountaineers (*gortsy*) fought collectivizers and labor recruiters from Grozny, who desperately needed able-bodied men for the petroleum industry. At the same time, the NKVD reported that hundreds of illegal armed Chechen groups operated in the Caucasus, sometimes engaging in pitched battles with NKVD units.[18] Some historians have argued that a major source of Soviet violence was the overwhelming need for homogeneity from the center and an antagonism toward genuine autonomy, real cultural difference, and idiosyncratic arrangements of any kind. Stalin's attacks on these non-Russian peoples can be partly explained in this framework.

Already in the late 1930s, Stalin began a campaign to extol the virtues of the Great Russian people. History books reversed the earlier Soviet condemnation of Russian imperialism in Central Asia and the Caucasus and increasingly lauded the Russian nation for bringing civilization and development to the backward peoples of the Russian Empire. Soviet patriotism, as it developed during the war, tried to absorb the experience of the subject nations into that of the Russians. Numerous non-Slavic soldiers served shoulder to shoulder with Russians, Belorussians, and Ukrainians, learning Russian for the first time, while taking great pride in common victories. But any nation that stood in the way of the melding of Soviet and Russian patriotism was imperiled. The deportations of the peoples of the northern Caucasus and Crimea in 1944 can be understood only in this context.

As usual, Stalin and Beria used security issues as the justification for deporting the peoples of the northern Caucasus, whom they accused of collaborating, or at least sympathizing with, the Nazis during their invasion of the Soviet Union.[19] No doubt Stalin and Beria were convinced of Chechen and Ingush treachery. In concise, factual communications, Beria described to Stalin the efficient, military-like assault on the Chechens and Ingush that began on the night of February 23–24, 1944. "According to your orders," the mission was accomplished, wrote Beria, making it clear to posterity that this action took place on Stalin's initiative.[20] The entire Chechen and Ingush nations, 496,460 men, women, and children, party members and heroes of the Soviet Union, as well as simple sheep-herders, oil workers, and mountaineers, were rounded up in a matter of days and deported first in guarded trucks to railheads and then in sealed trains, often little more than cattle cars, to Kazakhstan and Kirghizia.

As was so often the case in the history of forced deportations, there was a very high rate of mortality during the transport itself. Some ten thousand Chechens and Ingush died en route. There was little food or water available to the deportees, and the conditions of sanitation were primitive and inhuman. Periodically, the trains would halt by the sidings and the dead bodies would be thrown out of the train cars and quickly buried (and sometimes not) before the trains continued on the deadly trek. NKVD medical officials complained that normal provisions for the health and welfare of the deportees were completely lacking. When the trains arrived at their destinations and the survivors were transported to the special settlements that were to accommodate them, the familiar story prevailed: there were no supplies to build shelters, no food to fill their bellies, and no tools to begin work. The local Kazakhs, themselves in no shape to provide help to anyone, refused to allow the Chechens and Ingush into their kolkhozes and scattered settlements. The deportees had to scrape in the dirt for food, were beset by the spread of typhus, and died—according to Chechen and Ingush historians—by the hundreds of thousands, up to 40 percent of the population. NKVD data indicate that between 20 and 25 percent of the Chechens and Ingush died during the first four years of exile, with child mortality higher than the rest.[21]

We know that Stalin ordered the operation and Beria carried it out. We also know that the Chechens and Ingush were scattered throughout the Kazakh population for the purpose of denationalizing them, if not eliminating them as people. Chechen and Ingush historians to this day consider this a case of genocide. There is much to recommend their assertion. The land of the Chechens was to be repopulated by other nationalities; the Chechen and Ingush culture was to vanish in the steppes of Kazakhstan. At the very least, then, this was a case of attempted cultural genocide. Even after 1956, when Nikita Khrushchev rehabilitated many of the other "punished peoples" in his speech at the Twentieth Party Congress and allowed them to return to their homelands, the Chechens and Ingush were told they were to remain in exile. However, they paid no attention to Khrushchev's distinctions and began to return home on their own, sometimes even fighting their way back to the northern Caucasus, where they continue to resist Moscow's control to this day.

The story was very similar for the Crimean Tatars, though in this case there were both better reasons to doubt the Tatars' loyalty and genuine military-political concerns about the Tatar presence in the strategically vulnerable Crimean peninsula. Once again, the entire nation was deported in a military-style operation in May 1944 to Central Asia and the Urals. The transport was brutal, and the length of the trip to Kirghizia and Tadzhikistan killed many thousands of deportees. The Tatars' situation in Kirghizia was little better than that of the Chechens and Ingush in Kazakhstan. It is estimated that out of 190,000 Crimean Tatars, 70,000 to 90,000 died in transit or in the first years of exile. Like the Chechens and Ingush—as well as Balkars, Karachevtsy, and Kalmyks—the Crimean Tatars were told that they were exiled "in perpetuity" and "without the right to return to their previous place of residence."[22] After 1956 the Tatars were also forbidden to return to their homeland in the Crimea but, like the Chechens and Ingush, they did so in any case. Now in Ukraine, the Tatars of the Crimea continue to fight for the right to reclaim their lands, most of which were resettled after their deportation with Russian and Ukrainian peasants.

Stalin's nationality policy in the 1930s and 1940s was a contradictory mix of high-flown promises of cultural and economic development and state demands for conformity and submission. On the one hand, Soviet authorities continued the processes of *korenizatsiia*—building national allegiance among ethnic groups whose historical identities had been much more fluid and had revolved around demarcations of clan, religion, region, occupation, and language. On the other hand, some ethnicities were culturally eliminated because they were seen as too small and irrational, while others were singled out as "enemies" and sent into exile with the idea that they would disappear through a combination of attrition, permanent removal from their homelands, and assimilation into their new surroundings.

6 THE GREAT TERROR

In his pioneering work on the purges of 1937–38, Robert
Conquest coined the term "the Great Terror," and it has
continued to be used by historians ever since.[1] The term
captures well the "apocalyptic theater of horrors" of those
two years in which every Soviet citizen, with the exception of the *vozhd'* himself—Stalin—could potentially be
arrested, tortured, exiled, or executed.[2] The fear was pal-
pable and, especially for those in any position of responsibility— the nomenklatura of the party, factory bosses,
intellectuals, army generals, and newspaper editors—bags
were packed in case the knock on the door came at night.

The atmosphere in the major cities and provincial centers was tense; there was a kind of powerlessness about
one's situation that left everyone gasping for air. It would
be hard for anyone who did not experience the fear and
helplessness, the denunciations and confessions, to understand what it was like to live through that period. "I have
seen faces consumed, glimpsed horror under lowered eye-
lids, cheeks etched with pain," wrote Anna Akhmatova in
the poem "Requiem," her moving attempt to describe the

terrible experience of trying to find her arrested son during this period.

Yet, interestingly and instructively, when we try to imagine Soviet life in the Stalinist 1930s, people continued to do what they had always done: entertaining movies were made and watched; theater performances were packed with eager audiences; young men and women participated in mass physical culture demonstrations; and people marveled at the accomplishments of Soviet fliers and polar explorers.[3] "Life has become better, comrades," Stalin wrote in 1935. "Life has become more joyous." And this was not simply rhetoric, at least not for some members of the elite. Soviet jazz became wildly popular; swing dancing was all the rage. Comedic musicals dominated the film screens.[4]

The purges of 1937–38 are hard to classify as genocide because no particular ethnic, social, or political groups were attacked, though alleged political opponents, most of whom ended up being executed, were indeed placed together by their accusers in completely fabricated conspiratorial parties. The major figures of Bolshevism became the chief defendants in three show trials: the Trial of the 16 or the "Trotskyite-Zinovievite Terrorist Center" in August 1936; the Trial of the 17 or the "Anti-Soviet Trotskyite Center" in January–February 1937; and the Trial of the 21 or the "Anti-Soviet Bloc of Rights and Trotskyites" in March 1938. At the first trial, Zinoviev and Kamenev, among others, confessed to having organized the assassination of Kirov (December 1, 1934) and having conspired with Trotsky to murder Stalin and other leading members of the party. In the second trial, Piatakov and Radek admitted that they had engaged in widespread wrecking and sabotage, including the undermining of the railway system in connivance with Trotsky and the Japanese. As Wladislaw Hedeler writes: "In memorizing what was dictated to them by their NKVD interrogators, the defendants regurgitated the new version of party history" that had been rewritten "to comply with Stalin's megalomania and infallibility."[5]

Bukharin and Rykov were the major figures of the third show trial (Tomsky had committed suicide in September 1936). These leading figures of the so-called Right Opposition were accused of organizing "wrecking, diversionist, and terrorist activities," with the goal of provoking an invasion of the Soviet Union for the purpose of dismantling the socialist system and restoring capitalism.[6] All three groups put on trial were accused of working for a "central group" of Trotskyites and rightists that represented the interests of Trotsky and foreign governments in the Soviet Union. In fact, Trotsky was the major defendant in absentia at the Moscow show trials. His alleged confederates confessed to their crimes, and most were shot right away. An NKVD agent killed Trotsky in Mexico with a pickax to the head in August 1940. Vyshinsky's closing speech at the Bukharin trial (March 11, 1938) summed up his satisfaction with the elaborate trial extravaganza that he had directed:

The whole country, from the youngest to the oldest, are waiting for and demanding one thing: that the traitors and spies who sold out our motherland to the enemy be shot like vile dogs. The people demand one thing: that the accursed vermin be squashed! Time will pass. The hated traitors' graves will become overgrown with weeds and thistles, covered with the eternal contempt of honest Soviet people, of the entire Soviet people. While over our happy land, bright and clear as ever, our sun will shine its rays. We, our people, will as before stride along our path now cleansed of the last trace of the scum and vileness of the past, led by our beloved leader and teacher, the great Stalin.[7]

The trial transcripts, the defendants' self-abasement and confessions, and the brutality of the prosecutor and the Soviet state toward their "founding fathers" have been known to students of the Soviet Union for decades. Bukharin's "confession" has been deconstructed by scholars to demonstrate the fact that he turned the accusations on their head, admitting to all of the self-contradictory, absurd charges as a way to show that none of them could be true. But there is also plenty of evidence to demonstrate that Bukharin was a beaten and thoroughly humiliated man, who confessed so completely because he could not take any more abuse from the party-state he had worked so hard to create. We know a lot about the fearsome browbeating, torture, and threats to family members that lay behind many of the confessions. That Stalin directed the trials behind the scenes is not a matter of historical dispute. He systematically eliminated his chief political rivals through this process of trials, confession, and execution.

What is less well known is how long and methodical were the preparations for these events. In some senses, Zinoviev and Kamenev, Radek and Piatakov, and Bukharin, Rykov, and Tomsky were tried by the party in lengthy proceedings long before their arrests and show trials in front of Soviet and world public opinion. The newly available transcripts of the Central Committee plenum and Politburo meetings in the early 1930s demonstrate that Stalin and his close allies—Molotov, Kaganovich, Voroshilov, Mikoyan, and Kuibyshev, not to mention Yagoda and Yezhov—conducted ongoing cross-examinations of these major figures of the Bolshevik past, repeatedly forcing them on the defensive, seeking weaknesses and inconsistencies in their rebuttals. Constantly fed with new materials from brutal interrogations of minor party members by the OGPU/NKVD, Stalin's henchmen were able to outflank the best arguments of the Old Bolshevik elite.

In these discussions, the Mafia-like quality of the Bolshevik "family" played itself out in brutal and painful confrontations between accused and accusers. The *padrone*, Stalin, sat and watched in the background, interjecting himself into the squabbles at will, often with his typically sarcastic humor. Sometimes his interpellations were forceful and direct and ended the conversation; sometimes he acted as the dispassionate arbiter, restraining his more aggressive comrades.

The "defendants" were in an extremely difficult position in these Central Committee and Politburo confrontations, as they tried to use reasoned argument and honest denial (and, in Tomsky's case, humor and jokes) to stave

off threats to remove them from their positions in the
Central Committee and in the government. As the attacks
intensified, the veteran Bolsheviks became increasingly
aware that much more was at stake than their jobs and
reputations; they had to fight for their lives and those of
their families as the accusations spread to those of wrecking and treason.

Despite months, even years, of this kind of political assault, things could also change drastically from one day
to the next. The case of Yagoda was typical. First, while
Yagoda was increasingly maligned by his comrades in the
Central Committee, Yezhov was moved into an important
position in the NKVD to keep an eye on him and assume
some of his powers. Then Yezhov replaced him as chief of
the NKVD and Yagoda was appointed head of the People's
Commissariat of Communications. Finally, Stalin sent the
order (March 31, 1937) to have Yagoda arrested: "The
Politburo . . . thinks it necessary to exclude him from Politburo and TsK. The Politburo . . . would like to inform
the members of the TsK VKP, that in view of the danger
of leaving Yagoda in freedom for even one more day, it
considers it necessary to give the order to immediately arrest Yagoda. The Politburo . . . requests the members of
the Central Committee to sanction the exclusion of Yagoda
from the party and the TsK and his arrest."[8]

Before directly attacking the old Bolshevik icons, Stalin
and his lieutenants would go after smaller fry, as a way to
tarnish the reputations and motives of their more senior
protectors in the hierarchy. In the joint session of the Politburo and the Presidium of the Central Party Control Com-

mission of November 27, 1932, the "Group of Smirnov, Eismont, and Tolmachev" was excoriated for loose and drunken talk about problems of the party leadership during the collectivization campaign. But even more central to the goals of exposing the "affair" was Stalin's ongoing attack on the "rightists" Rykov and especially the popular Tomsky and their prestige and party base. At this point, Rykov and Tomsky were only reprimanded, while the others were expelled from the Central Committee.[9] But the accusations that came up in these internal party cross-examinations were used later during NKVD interrogations and forced confessions.

The attacks on Rykov and Tomsky were sustained and vicious; those on Bukharin had a particularly poignant quality since he had been the "darling of the party" and a favorite of Lenin's. As the assaults mounted, Bukharin increasingly could feel the ground beneath him turn to quicksand. The "confessions" of Zinoviev and then of Radek made Bukharin's position in the party—once seemingly unassailable—all the more difficult. He was pushed, bullied, and heckled by his Central Committee comrades, yet he continued to try to take the high road, though with little success. When he was finally arrested on January 27, 1937, he denied the charges of treason, terrorism, and planning the overthrow of the Soviet government. To the end, he protested his love of Stalin and the party leadership.

That Bukharin and others were accused of participating in conspiracies involving completely incompatible political opposites was no chance occurrence. Tactically, from the point of view of the authorities, this gave the groups greater ability to harm the state, while Stalin's drive to eliminate all of them, the supposed Left and Right, was all the greater. As Robert Tucker has written, Stalin was not just a paranoid who believed that individuals were out to get him. He suffered from a "paranoid delusional system," meaning that his opponents were joined together in interconnected groups, manipulated from abroad by Trotsky and his son Lev Sedov, as well as by foreign governments. Tucker writes: "Authorities describe a paranoid system as an intricate, schematized, and logically elaborated structure with a 'central delusional theme' involving a hostile plot of which the person concerned is an intended victim."[10] In essence, an entire mythological structure of traitors and spies was constructed to satisfy the boss's fantasies. The more unlikely the members of the same groups, the more Stalin and the NKVD could convince themselves and their associates that everyone was potentially dangerous. Paradoxically, the less likely the conspiracies, the more ubiquitous they became.

There can be no question that Stalin was in charge of this insane witch hunt for enemies and traitors. Across the board, Stalin was a micromanager of Soviet international and domestic affairs, and most particularly in those cases when state security was involved. Especially in those periods when the OGPU/NKVD were involved in purges, trials, terror, and executions, Stalin met with his security chiefs frequently, sometimes more than once a day.[11] Yagoda's OGPU had been condemned as insufficiently vigilant, unable to grasp the extent of the treachery, indeed even participating in it. In the view of Stalin and the Soviet leadership, countless "two-faced" party members, those who vociferously supported Stalin and the Soviet state on the surface but in fact worked as spies and agents for foreign powers, had infiltrated the machinery of the state, conducting industrial espionage and undermining Soviet institutions. They had to be chased down, the "truth" extracted from them one way or another, and sentenced to death. Georgi Dimitrov records in his diary a toast that Stalin gave at a lunch at Voroshilov's (November 7, 1937), in response to a toast that had been raised to the Great Stalin.

> Whoever attempts to destroy that unity of the socialist state, whoever seeks the separation of any of its parts of nationalities—that man is an enemy, a sworn enemy of the state and peoples of the USSR. And we will destroy each and every such enemy, even if he was an old Bolshevik; we will destroy all his kin, his family. We will mercilessly destroy anyone who, by his deeds or thoughts—yes, his thoughts—threatens the unity of the socialist state. To the complete destruction of all enemies, themselves, and their kind! (Approving exclamations: To the Great Stalin!)[12]

As a result, Stalin put Yezhov, "the mad dwarf" (in Khrushchev's characterization), in charge of the NKVD in September 1936, and Yezhov proceeded to purge Yagoda and his clientele in the NKVD and elsewhere in the apparatus. Yezhov himself was as vile a perpetrator as one will find in the history of modern genocide.[13] He was a drunkard and dissolute, despite his intellectual pretensions and contacts, and he personally participated in the interrogation and torture of his victims. He was also mesmerized by Stalin and conformed completely to his master's wishes to spread terror and killing throughout Soviet society, sparing no one. Like Stalin, Yezhov was known to justify the execution of many innocent people if the trade-off was to catch the guilty ones. His speech in the election campaign of December 1937 underlines his genocidal character:

> During their struggle [against the Soviet people], this whole disgusting band of Trotskyist-Bukharinist degenerates play the most dirty, fishy, monstrous tricks on us, in order somehow to call a halt to the triumphant advance of our people toward communism. Our further success to a high degree will depend on our ability to identify these clever methods of the class enemy against us, on our will to at least cleanse the Soviet country of this vermin. . . . Our Soviet people will exterminate to a man all these despicable servants of the capitalist lords, vile enemies of all workers.[14]

Yezhov was also determined to crush the families of the accused. He issued orders "to confine all wives of condemned traitors" and to arrest any of their children over fifteen years of age as "socially dangerous."[15]

The executions of the primary defendants of the Moscow show trials and the repression of their families, friends, acquaintances, and alleged accomplices were only the tip of the iceberg of the Great Terror. Yezhov drew up a plan, complete with quotas, for arresting "enemies of the people" who allegedly threatened the existence of the country. In 1937 and 1938 the NKVD arrested some 1,575,000 people, the vast majority of whom were brought to "trial." Of those, 681,692 people were executed, while the rest were assigned to exile and potential death in the Gulag.[16] The number of victims is likely to be much higher in both cases.[17] These were mostly ordinary people, workers, peasants, unemployed, petty criminals, civil servants of the lower order, few of whom had any opportunity, much less intent, to commit treasonous acts. Once they were identified by the police as enemies and swept up into the system of repression, they had little hope of release.

The very extent of the killing and repression lends weight to the argument that one could call this genocide instead of the normal appellation of "terror." After all, we speak confidently about the Cambodian "genocide," which had many of the same characteristics as the Great Terror: a party leader—Pol Pot—turning against his own party leadership and its history, as well as survivors of the prior regime, and persecuting intellectuals and those who thought for themselves, in the name of a "clean slate." Pol Pot also attacked national minorities, as did Stalin. On the other hand, the Cambodian genocide involved a far larger percentage of Cambodian citizens than did Stalin's repressions. If not genocide, the Great Terror was, write Jörg Baberowski and Anselm Doering-Manteuffel, "a Soviet variant of the 'final solution'," or, in Ronald Suny's estimation, "a political holocaust."[18]

Even though there was unambiguous direction from the top of the Soviet hierarchy and from Stalin above all, the purges of 1937–38—including Order 00447—did indeed take on a life of their own. The initiatives of Soviet officials in the Great Terror, as well as in dekulakization, the Ukrainian terror famine, the attack on nationalities, the "cleansing" of the cities, and other actions, were in part the result of a Soviet version of "working toward the Führer," the concept developed in the historiography of Nazism to explain the activism of Nazi bureaucrats, particularly in the killing of the Jews, in the absence of direct orders from Hitler. Soviet officials understood Stalin's bloodlust in this period and did more than their part in satisfying it. At the same time, the victims of NKVD interrogations implicated wide networks of people, who in turn named further circles of accomplices to satisfy their persecutors. Like quotas in the Soviet economic system, those set for numbers of arrested in the provinces were "met and surpassed" by overzealous local officials.

There were devastating competitions between rival NKVD hierarchs, who sought to prove their worth to Yezhov and Stalin by arresting and executing even more "enemies" than called for in their plans. Regularly, they asked permission from Yezhov to increase the numbers in their quotas, especially for those in the "first category," to be executed. Since very, very few of those seized by the NKVD were *really* guilty of any crime against the state, it was easy enough to widen the circles of those implicated. Yet one has to be careful with the official figures for arrests and executions. To win favor, some Soviet officials, especially in the periphery, would inflate the numbers of prosecutions and convictions as a way to curry favor with the bosses.

"Troikas" and "dvoikas"—hastily assembled local judicial bodies composed of representatives from the NKVD, the Justice Ministry, and the party—did their work quickly and efficiently of "trying" those brought before them by the NKVD. According to one estimate, some 800,000 people were executed over sixteen months, at a rate of 50,000 executions per month, or 1,700 per day for nearly 500 days.[19] All of this was carried out with the highest level of secrecy. The victims were taken to nearby NKVD-administered forests and then shot and buried in unmarked graves. The executioners—almost all NKVD officers—were told not to say a word about the events and even to "forget" what they had seen and done, on pain of severe punishment themselves. The sculpting of Soviet society was to take place without leaving any traces of the extraneous material that was cut away. Relatives were not informed of the fate of their loved ones; they were told either nothing at all or unfounded stories about terms of exile in unidentified places or about deaths in the camps.

In all of these extraordinary judicial processes and killing, there was a strange mixture of secrecy and publicity. The show trials highlighted the extent to which Stalin wanted the public to know about the treachery of many of their political leaders. Meanwhile, others were tried in secret and shot without any notification. But sometimes even the secret tribunals were designed to serve Stalin's agitational purposes. On June 11, 1937, as Central Committee

secretary, he sent the following note to all of the party national central committees, regional committees, and provincial committees (*natskom, kraikom, obkom*) regarding the leadership of the Red Army: "In connection with
the ongoing trial of the spies and enemies Tukhachevskii,
Yakir, Uborevich and others, the TsK recommends to you
that you organize meetings of workers and, where possible,
peasants, and also meetings of Red Army units and pass
resolutions about the necessity of carrying out the highest
measures of repression [the death sentence.] The notifi-
cations about the sentences will be published tomorrow,
that is, June 12."[20] But even in less important cases, Stalin
wanted the public to know the fate of alleged enemies. He
wrote to the Smolensk *obkom* secretary in August 1937: "I
recommend that you sentence the enemies of Andreevskii
region to be shot, and to publicize the shooting in the local
press."[21] What was at work was Stalin's perverse conviction that the common folk—workers, peasants, youth, and
others—would believe that his government was doing a
vigilant job of uncovering the misdeeds of the wreckers
and spies who were responsible for the impossibly hard
lives the Soviet people had to endure.

Torture, of course, was a very effective means of ex-
tracting denunciations of others, not to mention detailed
confessions, from completely innocent victims. One nasty
case of torture, that of the famous theater producer, director, and innovator Vsevolod Meyerhold, will have to stand
for a whole generation of torture victims, especially since
archival materials on the methods, forms, and "science"
of NKVD torture, if they exist, have not been made avail-

able to researchers. Meyerhold was able to send a letter to Molotov, which has survived, protesting his imprisonment and torture by the NKVD in 1939.

When the investigators began to apply to me physical methods they beat me, a sick, old man of sixty-five. They placed me on the floor, face down; they beat me with a rubber whip on my heels and back. When I sat on a bench, they used the same rubber whip to beat me from above, with great force. In the days that followed, when these parts of my legs hemorrhaged profusely, they again beat these red-blue-yellow blood-filled places with the same rubber whip and the pain was such that it seemed they were pouring on these sick, sore areas intensely boiling water, and I screamed and cried from pain. They beat my back with this rubber; they beat me by hand on the face, swinging from above. . . . They combined this with a so-called psychic attack. The one and the other aroused in me such monstrous fear that my personality was stripped to its very roots. . . . Lying on the floor with my face down, I twisted, contorted, and howled like a dog whom its owner beats with a lash. . . .

I lay down on my cot and fell asleep only in order an hour later to be led again to the interrogation, which previously had lasted eighteen hours, awakened by groans and by having tossed on the cot like a sick man dying of fever. "Death (yes, of course!), death is easier than this?" is what one person under

investigation said to himself. I, too, told myself this.
And I began to slander myself in the hope that they
would lead me to the scaffold.[22]

Meyerhold confessed to being a British and Japanese spy
and was executed in February 1940.

The matter of torture is separate from, though related
to, that of genocide. The willingness of the authorities to
use these vicious and inhuman methods against a substantial number of people, without any hesitation, qualms, or
regrets, indicates the kind of murderousness that prompts
cases of genocide. In some sense, there is no genocide
without systematic torture, though, of course, one can
easily identify cases of torture in which genocide is not
at play. There is plenty of evidence that Stalin not only
knew about the horrors and extent of NKVD torture, he
also encouraged it. In one case, Stalin ordered Yezhov to
extract a confession from an accused one way or the other:
"Isn't it time to squeeze this gentleman and force him to
report on his dirty little business. Where is he: in a prison
or a hotel." On one of the arrest lists that Yezhov routinely
sent to Stalin, the *rozhd'* jotted down by the name of M. I.
Baranov, "beat, beat!"[23] Stalin believed, as he already
noted at the Seventeenth Party Congress in January 1934,
that though the Soviet state had "smashed the enemies of
the party, the opportunists of all shades, [and] the nationalist deviators of all kinds," the "remnants of their ideology still live in the minds of individual members of the
party, and not infrequently find expression."[24] The only
way to get these "two-faced" party members to confess
their real thinking was to beat it out of them.

In the Soviet setting, there was widespread fear that arrest and interrogation meant torture, though by no means was this always the case. In this way, the very threat of torture itself became a means of social control and information gathering. Faced not just with the possibility of arrest, interrogation, and exile, but with that of horrendous physical abuse, Soviet officials easily found ways to report on their rivals and bosses for deficiencies in their administrations or industries. In doing so, they attempted to avoid responsibility and thus the likelihood of arrest and potential torture themselves. If the NKVD investigators translated these denunciations into invented stories about the spying and treason of colleagues and friends at work, the accusers were all too willing to go along with them.

Yezhov personally participated in torture sessions and reported on the outcomes directly to Stalin. Historians have found documents in which Stalin indicates to Yezhov that "physical means" of interrogation should be used. But Yezhov frequently demonstrated his own initiative when it came to torture, arrest, and executions.[25] In this sense, like the purges themselves, torture was institutionalized by a system that needed to search out and find enemies, in order to justify its very existence and find excuses for its failings. The case of Marshal Mikhail Tukhachevskii, the central figure in the widespread purge of the Red Army, is typical in this connection. Yezhov later revealed that the question of torture had come up at the highest levels when discussing how to make the widely respected marshal confess. The chief prosecutor Vyshinskii demanded that he be tortured. Stalin essentially gave the go-ahead to Yezhov: "See for yourself, but

Tukhachevskii should be forced to tell everything and to reveal his contacts. It is impossible that he acted on his own." Stalin was daily informed by Yezhov of the progress of the interrogation, which during the Khrushchev years was revealed to have been quite bloody. On June 11, 1937, Tukhachevskii and seven of the leading army generals were condemned to death by a military tribunal for treason and spying. Soon thereafter nearly a thousand additional high-ranking military officers and political commissars were arrested and purged.[26] Torture did its job, as Stalin knew it would.

The extreme contrast between the utopianism of Marxism-Leninism-Stalinism as practiced in the 1930s, an ideology that promised the victory of socialism, the creation of a new Soviet man and woman, and the perfection of life itself, and the realities of deprivation, famine, cramped living quarters, and poorly compensated labor created the systemic need for purges and violence. Some historians have also pointed out the problematic relationship between the center and the periphery as a source for the purges. More tenable than this assertion, now pretty much disproven, that the purges originated in the regions, is the argument that Stalin wanted to shake up local state and party satraps, killing some, exiling others, while promoting a new generation of more pliant cadres.[27]

Whether in the provinces or in the capital, the purges fit Stalin's need for unassailable power. For Stalin, there were too many Old Bolsheviks around, veterans of the revolution, who felt entitled to their positions and privileges and thus might challenge his leadership or at least stall his policies. And not just Stalin was interested in expanding his power and getting even with his enemies. The purges unleashed a torrent of denunciations, as middle- and lower-level party and state officials settled scores by informing on their rivals and opponents. Careerism promoted some of this reporting; some was meant defensively—if I don't report first on Comrade Ivanov, he will report on me. But, in the end, the NKVD had more than enough information to spread its net of arrests and investigations even without torture and repeated interrogations.

Stalin and the NKVD encouraged denunciations, arrests, and trials at all levels of society. Everyone was to have a stake in identifying and eliminating supposed enemies. The population would be mobilized in this manner and taught to engage in a system that left no citizen out of the drama of creating a new Soviet society. On behalf of the Central Committee, Stalin wrote to the local party chiefs (August 3, 1937): "Considering completely necessary the political mobilization of kolkhozniks around the work carried on to destroy the enemies of the people in agriculture . . . , [the Central Committee] orders you to organize in every region by locality open show trials against enemies of the people, wreckers in agriculture . . . widely publicizing the course of the trials in the local press."[28] In particular, Stalin was anxious to have the kolkhoz farmers aroused against those local officials who supposedly undermined the success of Soviet agriculture. The same would apply to factory workers, who should know about the wrecking activities of their supervisors.

There was method to Stalin's madness: the attack of the NKVD on the Soviet population was not completely random. Biography and genealogy mattered and mattered a lot, as the work of Oleg Khlevniuk, the premier Russian historian of the purges, has demonstrated.[29] Old Bolsheviks and their allies, families, contacts, and friends fell to the sword of the NKVD and Stalin, as did the leading military officers of the Red Army, especially those who had participated in the Civil War and had an independent sense of self as worthy founders of Soviet power. Clearly, Stalin worried about the threat of "Bonapartism" in the ranks of the Red Army, though again, there is little evidence that these fears were in any way founded in reality. Former Mensheviks, Socialist Revolutionaries, and Kadets, among other non-Bolshevik political formations, also did not stand much of a chance of escaping arrest and its horrific consequences. These and other potential political opponents—and the people associated with them in any way—constituted an important target of the purge machinery.

Equally important (and more numerous) were those targeted because of their social background: kulaks, priests, ex-landowners, ex-tsarist officials, "asocials," and so on. In addition to the terrible fate of the kulaks, the devastating attack on Russian priests, nuns, and monks in the 1930s, which saw tens of thousands executed and sent into exile, might also be considered a genocidal action. As we saw earlier, national as well as social background mattered, as especially Poles and Germans, but also French, English, Greeks, Finns, and others, were rounded up by the NKVD and exiled or executed. According to data on the Great Terror, in fact, the largest single group of "repressed" consisted of nationalities with "homelands" abroad and foreigners.

But we could go too far in seeing the purges as a rational, if exaggerated, response to potential opposition. Many in the categories above escaped being purged. In fact, some scholars of the period have noted that it was precisely from these targeted groups that Stalin recruited some of his closest confederates; their very vulnerability was a tested way to ensure their loyalty. Even more important to understanding the arbitrariness of the terror is the fact that no one was safe from arrest; hundreds of thousands of ordinary Soviet citizens, in the party and out, with "clean" social, political, and national biographies, ended up under arrest, executed, or in exile. When Beria effectively replaced Yezhov in November 1938, and proceeded to execute him and his lieutenants in the NKVD for excesses in the carrying out of the purges, it was precisely the innocence of so many of the arrested and the "illegal methods" that were used to extract confessions, to which the documents averred. Beria's record, of course, proved to be little better than Yezhov's.

David Shearer makes the important point that the purges did little to improve the performance or efficiency of Soviet institutions. On the contrary, the judiciary, police, and military organizations were in shambles as a result. The purging of industrial elites increased the incidence of factory accidents and production snafus. The railway system was left in chaos as a result of the top to bottom purge of the railway administration and railway workers.[30] The party was also decapitated of its leadership, the vast majority of whom had been Bolsheviks before 1921. Of the 139 members and candidate members of the Central Committee of the party at the Seventeenth Party Congress in 1934, 98, or about 70 percent, were arrested and executed in 1937–38.[31]

The dangers to Soviet security from beyond the USSR's borders and the increasingly tense international situation, to a large extent caused by Hitler's successful bullying of the European powers, are said to have been the primary motivation for the terror and purges. As Oleg Khlevniuk writes: "The NKVD orders guiding the mass operations in 1937–38 show that the Great Terror was a centrally organized punitive action, planned in Moscow, against a potential fifth column perceived as capable of stabbing the country in the back in case of war."[32] But the arrests and mass killing during the purges were driven less by the real threats to Soviet security than by Stalin's xenophobia and paranoia. Without Stalin, the genocidaire, it is hard to imagine the Great Terror.

7 THE CRIMES OF STALIN
AND HITLER

In the introduction to his book *The Harvest of Sorrow*, which examines the history of collectivization and the Ukrainian famine of 1932–33, Robert Conquest compares the crimes of Stalinism with those of Nazism: "Fifty years ago, as I write these words, the Ukraine and the Ukrainian, Cossack, and other areas to the east—a stretch of territory with some forty million inhabitants—was like one vast Belsen. A quarter of the rural population, men, women and children, lay dead or dying, the rest in various stages of debilitation with no strength to bury their families or neighbours. At the same time (as at Belsen), well-fed squads of police or party officials supervised the victims."[1]

In the *Black Book of Communism*, Stephane Courtois even more directly makes this connection: "the genocide of a 'class' may well be tantamount to the genocide of a 'race'." The death of a Ukrainian kulak child whom the Stalinist regime purposely sacrificed in the famine "is equal to" the death of a Jewish child in the Warsaw

Ghetto, who died as a result of Nazi-instigated starvation.[2] Here, Conquest would disagree. He believes (meaning he has "the primary feeling") that the Holocaust was essentially "worse" than Stalin's crimes.[3]

Victims of communism—whether Latvian deportees to the Gulag or Russian political prisoners in Kolyma in eastern Siberia, relatives of Polish officers shot at Katyn, or of Chechen schoolteachers who perished in Kazakh exile—have a hard time understanding the special character of the crimes of Hitler. The Yugoslav writer Danilo Kis (whose father was a Hungarian Jew) writes: "Should anyone tell you Kolyma was different from Auschwitz, tell him to go to hell."[4]

Yet from a historical perspective, which is not necessarily the same as that of the victim or the perpetrator, it seems evident, as stated above, that the Holocaust is the most extreme case of genocide in human history. This comes from the apocalyptic nature of the Nazi racial utopia, the complete helplessness of the Jews in face of the attack on their very existence as a people, the sheer extent of the killing, and the industrial nightmare of the gas chambers and ovens of the elimination camps. As Richard Evans writes, "There was no Soviet Treblinka, built to murder people on their arrival."[5] Therefore, Courtois's comparison between the death of a child by starvation in the Warsaw Ghetto and that of a child caught up in the Ukrainian famine is a false one when comparing the larger dimensions of the Holocaust to Soviet mass killing. The legitimate comparison is between the fate of the child in Auschwitz or Treblinka and that of a child in famine-stricken Ukraine or in the Gulag. The Ukrainian child in the Soviet country-side or the child in the Gulag had a chance to survive; the Jewish child in the death camps was condemned to death, even if there were scattered exceptions.

The basic revulsion at the Holocaust remains with us today and legitimately shapes our understanding of a variety of important political and moral issues. Precisely because the Soviet Union was largely responsible for winning the war against the Nazis and lost twenty-seven million lives in defeating the evil that brought the world Auschwitz and Babi Yar, there is considerable and understandable reticence to consider Soviet crimes in the same category as Nazi ones. But the Holocaust was neither the only case of genocide in recent history nor so singular that it cannot be compared with other egregious episodes of mass killing, like the Armenian, Rwandan, or Cambodian genocides. Genocide is the "crime of crimes" in international law, but there are "worse" historical cases of genocide and less horrendous ones.[6]

This brings us back to the question of whether Stalin's murderous attacks on peoples, groups, classes, political opponents, and his population as a whole qualify as genocide, "the crime of crimes." Some scholars prefer to sidestep the question by coining new terms—like "classicide," "democide," or "politicide"—that preserve the ethnic-, national-, and religious- based exclusivity of genocide, while making it clear that Stalin's crimes as a whole constituted mass murder.[7] Others will focus on Stalin's murderous deportations of the "punished peoples" during the war as that part of his repertoire of mass killing that can be classified as genocide.[8] Still others look at the NKVD's executions of twenty-two thousand interned Polish army officers and government officials in 1940, the Katyn forest massacre, as the best case against the Stalinist regime for genocide.[9]

Some scholars would prefer not to use the term of genocide at all in historical studies of mass killing, arguing that it is too closely linked to international judicial norms and thus to proclamations of guilty or innocent. The historians' task, they maintain, is to liberate their narratives about mass killing from legal language. Others decide not to use the term because of the proliferation of the claims to genocide by a variety of peoples and groups that seek to strengthen the legitimacy of their historical sufferings, thus debasing and invalidating genocide's original meaning. There are also scholars who object that the term has become excessively politicized, used to condemn some states and political systems, while justifying military intervention.[10] These objections all have some merit; it is too easy to misuse the term genocide for a variety of purposes that have nothing to do with scholarship. But it also does not make sense for historians to sequester themselves from the international conversation about genocide, whether about the past or about the present. History and international judicial norms are inextricably intertwined. The principled abstention from using the term genocide can serve politicized purposes as much as its application to specific historical circumstances.

Much of the tiptoeing around the problem of genocide when dealing with the litany of Stalinist mass crimes relates to the language of the keystone of genocide legislation: the Convention on the Prevention and Punishment of the Crime of Genocide, adopted by the U.N. General Assembly on December 9, 1948. Here genocide is famously defined as a variety of "acts committed with the intent to destroy, in whole or in part, a national, ethnical, racial or religious group, as such." This powerful idea of genocide took hold especially in the 1980s and 1990s in the international courts regarding crimes in former Yugoslavia (primarily of Serbs against Bosnian Muslims) and in Rwanda (Hutu against Tutsi). The growing body of scholarship in "genocide studies" has also been deeply influenced by the force of the convention and by the extraordinary impact of "Holocaust studies," which argue in their most radical formulations that the Holocaust was a uniquely horrible event in the history of mass killing and that, at the very least, the mass murder of ethnic groups or nations should be at the core of genocide. But perhaps it is time to stop asking the question whether the group that is being murdered "in whole or in part" is a national, ethnic, and religious group, or whether it is a social, political, or economic group. What is, after all, the difference when it comes to human life?

Finally, I would like to return to the question of comparing Nazi and Soviet crimes of mass killing prompted by Conquest's unforgettable image of Belsen and the Ukrainian famine. In Paul Hollander's introduction to the volume *From the Gulag to the Killing Fields*, a compendium of personal accounts of victims of repression in communist states, he suggests that while both Stalinist and Nazi mass killings could be classified under the rubric of genocide, he is not ready to allow them "moral equivalence."[11] One of the reasons, he opines, is that "Communist states did not attempt to eradicate, in a premeditated, systematic, and mechanized fashion, any particular ethnic group or class of people." The second reason is that "Communist regimes, unlike the Nazis, did not seek to murder children." The third is that Nazi racial categories were immutable, an "inescapable death sentence" for the victims of the Holocaust, the Jews, while Soviet categories constantly shifted and changed according to the leadership's particular needs at any given time.

Without seeking in any way to lessen the horrors of the Holocaust or of Nazi crimes against gypsies (Roma and Sinti), homosexuals, Poles, Russians, particularly Soviet POWs, or others, I would suggest that the history of genocide in Stalinist Russia and the Third Reich provides more material for similarity than for difference in Hollander's categories of comparison.[12] Dekulakization and the Ukrainian famine surely should be seen in turn as attempts by the Stalinist government to eliminate "a class of people" and anyone who seemed to support them. The Chechens and Ingush, the Crimean Tatars, and other "punished peoples" of the wartime period were, indeed, slated for elimination, if not physically, then as self-identifying nationalities. While there is no question that the Nazis intended to eliminate the Jews, it is also true that substantial numbers were able to emigrate from Germany and Austria before the attack on Poland in 1939. As has been well established, the systematic elimination of the Jews was precipitated in the main by the Nazi invasion of the Soviet Union in June 1941.

It is interesting that both Courtois and Hollander point to the fate of children as, in one case, indicating the commonalities and, in the other, the distinctions between the fate of victims of the Nazi and Stalinist regimes. A review of the Russian publication *Deti GULAGa* (Children of the Gulag), which documents the Soviet regime's treatment of the children of those designated as "enemies of the people," should leave few illusions about the horrendous fate of the offspring of the millions of fathers and mothers who were executed or deported to the camps.[13] Except for their periodic convictions in a number of categories of criminal offenses, some blatantly political, minors were usually not executed by the Soviet regime. But children of the "repressed" population were highly susceptible to disease, hunger, exposure, and various forms of exploitation while in transport, in "special settlements," in orphanages, and in work camps. They were often forcibly separated from their parents and then disappeared into the NKVD orphanages, which were often little better than prisons and work camps themselves. This *is* different from the fearsome Nazi elimination of Jewish children in the death camps and at thousands of sites of mass murder across Eastern Europe and Russia. In this sense, Courtois is wrong and Hollander is right.[14] But the agony and untimely deaths of children under the Stalinist regime should not be forgotten. The mortality rates of children are hard to quantify, since so many never made it to term or died soon after birth because of the horrid conditions of their mothers' "repression" and internment, but surely infanticide also should be included in an indictment of the Stalinist regime. The indifference of the Stalinist leadership to the suffering of children should not be eliminated from our consideration of Soviet crimes.

Hollander also focuses on the importance of the "immutability" of Nazi racial categories, while Soviet designations of the "enemy" changed depending on the time and circumstances and thus did not constitute the "inescapable death sentence" that was faced by the Jews. In the case of alleged "kulaks," Volga Germans or Chechens during the war, and Poles before the amnesty of July 1941, there were similar elements of "immutability" in their situations. If the Soviet regime did not pronounce death sentences on all their numbers, they were forced to live under the imminent threat of dying. At the same time, it is worth noting that thousands of Jews married to Gentiles did survive the war in Germany, and there were several thousand Jews serving in the Wehrmacht, almost until the end, just as some kulaks in the Gulag were allowed to join the Red Army's defense of the homeland, though most often in special punishment battalions. Moreover, Nazi racial designations about Slavs were highly confused and inconsistently applied. Himmler selected Polish children for "reclaiming" by the German race because they had blond hair and blue eyes and "looked" German; in many cases, Nazi categories of race were no more systematic than this. Meanwhile, the Soviets deported every single Chechen and Ingush they could find, nearly half a million people, whether serving with distinction in the Red Army or occupying an important party post in Moscow. They could do so because the nationality of Soviet citizens was systematically registered by the internal passport system. Both totalitarian killers—Nazi Germany and Stalinist Russia—were perpetrators of genocide, the "crime of crimes." Even with the fall of the Soviet Union, we know much more about the Nazi crimes than we do about the Soviet ones, about those who conceived and ordered them, those who carried them out, and those who suffered and died as a consequence. The crucial issue of intentionality and criminal culpability in the Soviet case can only be answered definitively when we have full access to Russian archives. But we know enough now to make the case that both systems—Stalinist and Nazi—were genocidal by their very character, meaning that their distinct combinations of charismatic leaders (in a Weberian sense), dictatorial powers, ideological motivations, and Promethean transformative aspirations, led them to use the mass killing of groups of their own citizens (and others) as a way to achieve the impossible future that defined their very essence.

Hitler's often-repeated prophecy that the Jews would pay if they brought about a world war against the Third Reich has been justifiably discarded as the real reason for his genocidal attack against the Jews. Though the claim had more of a base in fact, Stalin's frequent invocations of foreign attacks on the Soviet Union are taken more seriously by historians than they should be as a cause for the mass killing of the 1930s. In both cases, mass murder was systemic, while intimately linked to the particular psychologies of the leaders involved.

With the death of Hitler and the collapse of the Third Reich, the German state ceased to be a genocidal threat altogether. A new state emerged out of the ashes of the Nazi catastrophe and the strictures of Allied occupation, one that consciously and determinedly turned its back on its twentieth-century history of war and genocide.[15] With the death of Stalin, many of the fundamentals of the system remained, but the threat of genocide in the Soviet Union quickly dissipated. The Soviet system frightened itself with its capacity for killing masses of its own citizens. Khrushchev and his successors continued the practice of interning political opponents but rejected the Stalinist urge to kill them or others for their alleged or real opposition.

Conclusions

The Soviet regime under Stalin decimated its own population. Because of the availability of NKVD data, as flawed as they might be, the numerical losses are easier to summarize than the costs of Stalinism to society and the country as a whole, which is such a deep, difficult, and elusive subject that few scholars have dared to take it on. Using the NKVD figures, between the early 1930s and 1953 some 1.1–1.2 million Soviet citizens were executed, three quarters during the period 1937–38. Some 6 million Soviet citizens were deported to the special settlements; 1.5 million (25 percent) experienced an "untimely death." During that period, as well, 16 to 17 million Soviet citizens were imprisoned in forced labor, 3 million of them convicted of "counterrevolutionary" activities. Ten percent of labor camp victims perished in untimely fashion.[1] These figures do not include the 3–5 million of victims of the Ukrainian famine or of the massacres and executions of Poles, Baltic peoples, peasants who resisted collectivization, and nationalities who fought their deportations. Nor do they include those who died in transport to the special settlements and labor camps or were killed or died during preliminary investigations, detention, and interrogations.

This brief study has made the case that Stalin was the crucial figure in any calculus of mass killing and that genocide is the appropriate appellation for that killing. Perhaps the most useful way to end the book is to summarize the major points of this argument.

1. The origins of the term "genocide" in the writings of Raphael Lemkin and the development of the 1948 U.N. convention on the prevention and punishment of genocide do not preclude using the term to identify political and social groups as victims of genocide. Lemkin himself originally had this in mind in his work during the 1930s. Original drafts of the U.N. convention also mentioned the centrality of political and social groups. In the end, however, the Soviet Union exerted a powerful political influence on the making of the U.N. convention, to the point where one can claim that the exclusion of social and political groups should not be honored in rigid fashion. The subsequent development of international law in connection with the prosecution of genocide also leads to a more flexible use of the term for the "crime of crimes." After 1991 the Baltic nations, in particular, have applied international legal precedents to the Soviet case, indicting—and in some cases convicting—former Soviet officials of genocide.

2. Stalin was not born or raised to be a mass killer. His upbringing in the Caucasus and Georgia cannot explain the extreme violence that later characterized his rule over

the Soviet system. He became a genocidaire over time, and there were a number of important moments in that personal evolution, from his difficult family background and youth in Georgia, to his involvement in the revolutionary movement, his attachment to Lenin and Bolshevism, his experiences in the underground and in exile, his role in the revolution and especially in the Civil War, which presaged in some ways what came later, and his involvement in the struggle for power in the 1920s. Even the blood spilled in the collectivization campaign in the early 1930s contributed to the growing acceptance of mass killing by Stalin and his lieutenants. The cumulative effect of his biography and personality created in him a fierce anger and resentment of those who stood in his way and could be seen as criticizing his achievements. Once he launched unionwide programs of industrialization and collectivization, their inevitable failures were blamed on entire groups of the population with the same hatred and vindictiveness he harbored for his political opponents.

3. Dekulakization can be looked at as genocidal. During the collectivization campaign Stalin and the Soviet regime demonized the alleged social group known and identified as kulaks. They were set off from the rest of the peasant population as "enemies of the people" and were slated to be wiped out as a group. Their status was deemed inheritable, and their official portrayal was that of being less than human. Several tens of thousands were shot on the orders of troikas set up to try alleged resisters. Nearly two million were removed from their lands and sent off to

barely inhabitable territory in the Far North and Siberia. There, in special settlements, many hundreds of thousands died of hunger, exposure, overwork, and disease.

4. A final wave of dekulakization in 1937–38 overlapped with a general effort on the part of Stalin and the regime to do away with those groups designated as socially "alien" people—vagrants, criminals, the homeless, prostitutes, the chronically unemployed, ex-kulaks, former landlords, and imperial government servants—who did not belong in a perfectible state, the socialist USSR. They were to be quarantined from the "healthy" corpus of Soviet citizens and eliminated from the body politic. The murderous campaign against these supposed enemies can be linked to the promulgation of the Soviet constitution in 1936, trumpeting the achievement of socialism, and the election campaign to the Supreme Soviet, which was to confirm this victory at the ballot box. The infamous Order 00447 contained quotas of people to be summarily tried and executed. Others would be exiled to the special settlements, where many died. This can be considered a particular kind of genocide: of an identifiable group of social "others," who did not fit into Stalin's conception of the future Soviet socialist society.

5. The Ukrainian killer famine should be considered an act of genocide. There is enough evidence—if not overwhelming evidence—to indicate that Stalin and his lieutenants knew that the widespread famine in the USSR in 1932–33 hit Ukraine particularly hard, and that they were ready to see millions of Ukrainian peasants die as a result. They made no efforts to provide relief; they pre-

vented the peasants from seeking food themselves in the cities or elsewhere in the USSR; and they refused to relax restrictions on grain deliveries until it was too late. Stalin's hostility to the Ukrainians and their attempts to maintain their form of "home rule" as well as his anger that Ukrainian peasants resisted collectivization fueled the killer famine.

6. The attack on certain "enemy" nationalities in some cases took on genocidal characteristics. Early in the 1930s those nationalities that had ostensible homelands abroad—the Poles, Germans, and Koreans in particular— were separated out from the rest of the Soviet national groupings and deemed inherently dangerous to the Soviet state. In particular, the actions against the Poles, starting with mass deportations to the special settlements in 1934 and culminating in the arrests and deportations of 1939–40 and the Katyn massacre of June 1940, can be thought of as genocidal. In 1944, during the war, the Muslim peoples from the northern Caucasus and the Crimea were deported en masse to special settlements in Central Asia. In the process of deportation and resettlement a substantial percentage of these peoples (Chechens-Ingush and Crimean Tatars, in particular) died. The peoples involved consider Stalin's actions genocidal. There is certainly evidence that the Soviet regime took these actions in order to have these peoples disappear, if not physically as human beings, though that happened in untoward numbers, then as members of a distinct nationality. At the very least, the attacks against the Chechens-Ingush and Crimean Tatars should be considered attempted cultural genocide.

7. The Great Terror of 1937–38 also had genocidal qualities, if it cannot be labeled genocide itself, at least according to the letter of the U.N. genocide convention and to most historical criteria as well. Stalin and the Soviet regime created invented groups of alleged political enemies and everyone associated with them and had them tried, interrogated, tortured, and executed or exiled to the Gulag. Stalin understood at the time that many tens of thousands of innocent people would be killed in the destruction of the Old Bolsheviks, the communist elite, the officers' corps, and the *nomenklatura*, along with their families, friends, and associates. He did nothing to stem the spread of suspicion and denunciation that constantly produced new victims. On the contrary, he encouraged the terror, showed no concern for its innocent victims, and brought it to an end only when war seemed imminent.

8. Stalin and his lieutenants at the time and subsequently, often decades later, defended their attacks on all levels of Soviet society by claiming that the country needed to prepare for war. Nationalities, kulaks, and social outcasts were assailed as members of a potential fifth column. Stalin and his deputies accused their alleged political opponents of working for foreign governments and Trotsky, and of being ready to assassinate government officials and overthrow the Soviet government at the first sign of war. This book suggests that the "war fear" argument, though inherent in Marxist-Leninist-Stalinist ideology, was both exaggerated and exploited by the Stalinists to justify their murderous actions throughout the 1930s. Of course, Soviet security was increasingly endangered by

the rise of Nazi Germany and the aggression of the Japanese in Asia. But the Soviet leadership did not prepare for war by their mass killing actions. In fact, just the opposite is true: they critically weakened the country by engaging in them and may have caused even more deaths during the war as a result.

9. Stalin's culpability for mass murder is not unlike that of Hitler's. Without Stalin it is hard to imagine the genocidal actions of the 1930s, just as without Hitler the Holocaust is historically unimaginable. This does not mean that violence was not built into the Soviet system, or that anti-Semitic attacks would not have occurred if—in a wistful counterfactual—Hitler had died in 1936. For a number of reasons the Holocaust should be thought of as the worst case of genocide in the modern era. Nevertheless, the points of comparison between Stalin and Hitler, Nazism and Stalinism, are too many to ignore. Both were dictators who killed vast numbers of people on the European continent. Both chewed up the lives of human beings in the name of a transformative vision of Utopia. Both destroyed their countries and societies, as well as vast numbers of people inside and outside their own states. Both—in the end—were genocidaires.

NOTES

ACKNOWLEDGMENTS

1. Norman Naimark, "Revolution, Stalinismus, und Genozid," *Aus Politik und Zeitgeschichte* 44–45 (October 27, 2007): 14–20; Naimark, "Totalitarian States and the History of Genocide," *Telos*, no. 136 (Fall 2006): 10–25; Naimark, "Stalin and the Question of Soviet Genocide," in *Political Violence, Behavior, and Legitimation*, ed. Paul Hollander (New York: Palgrave Macmillan, 2008), pp. 39–49.

INTRODUCTION

1. See, for example, Dan Diner, *Cataclysms: A History of the Twentieth Century from Europe's Edge*, trans. William Templar (Madison: University of Wisconsin Press, 2008), pp. 182–186.

2. *Sto sorok besed c Molotovym: Iz dnevnika F. Chueva* (Moscow: "Terra," 1991), pp. 390, 416.

3. On the dearth of foreign intelligence as a result of the recall and arrest of agents in the field, Z. I. Passov, chief of the NKVD's foreign intelligence service, wrote: "in the period of the [Nazi] preparations for actions regarding the seizure of Austria [and] Czechoslovakia, the foreign section did not receive a

single agent's report from Germany, not any information what-
soever." *Lubianka: Stalin i glavnoe upravlenie gosbezopasnosti
NKVD 1937–1938*, ed. A. N. Iakovlev, comp. V. N. Khaustov,
V. P. Naumov, N. S. Plotnikova (Moscow: Mezhdunarodnyi fond
"Demokratiia," 2004), p. 7.

4. Alexander N. Yakovlev, *A Century of Violence in Soviet
Russia*, trans Anthony Austin (New Haven: Yale University
Press, 2002), p. 234.

CHAPTER 1. THE GENOCIDE ISSUE

1. Cited in Samantha Power, *A Problem from Hell: America
and the Age of Genocide* (NewYork: Basic Books, 2002), p. 521,
n. 6. Some of the material here on the history of genocide comes
from Power and from my essay "Totalitarian States and the History of Genocide," pp. 10–25. See also Amir Weiner, "Nothing
but Certainty" (comment on Eric Weitz), *Slavic Review* 61, 1
(Spring 2002): 45–46.

2. Raphael Lemkin, *Axis Rule in Occupied Europe: Laws
of Occupation, Analysis of Government Proposals for Redress*
(Washington, DC: Carnegie Endowment for Inernational Peace,
1944), p. 79.

3. Robert Conquest, *Reflections on a Ravaged Century* (New
York: Norton, 2000), pp. 150–152.

4. Anton Weiss-Wendt, "Hostage of Politics: Raphael Lemkin on 'Soviet Genocide'," *Journal of Genocide Research* 7, 4
(December 2005): 551–559.

5. Power, *A Problem from Hell*, p. 51.

6. Donald Bloxham, *Genocide on Trial: War Crimes Trials
and the Formation of Holocaust History and Memory* (Oxford:
Oxford University Press, 2001), p. 203.

7. Francine Hirsch, "The Soviets at Nuremberg: International Law, Propaganda, and the Making of the Postwar Order,"

American Historical Review (June 2008): 714. I owe many of the observations about Nuremberg to Hirsch's research.

8. Arkady Vaksberg, *Stalin's Prosecutor: The Life of Andrei Vyshinsky*, trans. Jan Butler (New York: Grove Weidenfeld, 1990), p. 259.

9. *New York Times*, April 7 and 13, 1948.

10. A. N. Trainin, *Bor'ba progressivnykh sil protiv unichtozheniia natisonal'nykh grupp i ras* (Moscow: Vsesoiuznoe obshchestvo po rasprostraneniiu polit. i nauchn. znanii, 1948), p. 11.

11. Cited in Victor Zaslavsky, *Class Cleansing: The Massacre at Katyn* (New York: Telos Press, 2009), p. 23.

12. Nehemiah Robinson, *The Genocide Convention: A Commentary* (New York: Institute of Jewish Affairs, 1960), pp. 17–18; see Resolution 96 (I) in appendix 1, pp. 121–122. My emphasis.

13. Ibid., appendix 2, p. 123, "Draft Convention Prepared by the Secretariat." My emphasis.

14. William A. Schabas, *Genocide in International Law: The Crimes of Crimes* (Cambridge: Cambridge University Press, 2000), p. 136, n. 219. My emphasis.

15. UN General Assembly, Sixth Committee, Third Session, Sixty-fourth Meeting, October 1, 1948, "Continuation of the Consideration of the Draft Convention on Genocide," pp. 12–19.

16. *New York Times*, November 19, 1948.

17. Ibid., October 16 and 21, 1948.

18. M. N. Andriukhin, *Genotsid—tiagchaishee prestuplenie protiv chelovechestva* (Moscow: Gosud. Izd. Iuridicheskoi literatury, 1961), pp. 85–86.

19. "Report of the Sixth Committee on the Draft Convention on Genocide," December 6, 1948, *Foreign Relations of the United States (FRUS)*, vol. 1 (1948), "Human Rights" (Washington, DC: U.S. Government Printing Office), p. 298.

20. Schabas, *Genocide in International Law*, pp. 134–135.

21. See A. N. Trainin, "Bor'ba s genotsidom kak mezhdu-narodnym prestupleniem," *Sovetskoe Gosudarstvo i Pravo*, no. 5 (May 1948): 1–16; and Andriukhin, *Genotsid-tiagchashee prestuplenie protiv chelovechestra*, pp. 72–93.

22. Mark Levene, *Genocide in the Age of the Nation State*, vol. 1: *The Meaning of Genocide* (London: I. B. Tauris, 2005), p. 80.

23. Some of these convictions have been successfully appealed in the European Court of Human Rights. See: Antonio Casses, "Balancing the Prosecution of Crimes against Humanity and Non-Retroactivity of Criminal Law: The *Kolk and Kislyiy v. Estonia* Case before the ECHR," *Journal of International Criminal Justice* 4 (2006): 410–418.

24. I take much of this material from the research of Lauri Mälksoo, "Soviet Genocide? Communist Mass Deportations in the Baltic States and International Law," *Leiden Journal of International Law*, no. 14 (2001): 757–787. See also John B. Quigley, *The Genocide Convention: An International Law Analysis* (Derbyshire, UK: Ashgate, 2006).

25. Daniel Feierstein, "National Security Doctrine in Latin America: The Genocide Question," in Donald Bloxham and A. Dirk Moses, eds. *The Oxford Handbook of Genocide Studies* (Oxford, England: Oxford University Press, 2010), pp. 500–501. Here, in a case against Miguel Osvaldo Etchecolatz, the Court provided a compelling analysis of why the genocide label should be used: "This [crime] was not done in a random or indiscriminate fashion, but with the intention of destroying a section of the population. . . . composed of those citizens who did not fit the type pre-established by the promoters of the repression as necessary for the new order to be installed in the country." Thanks to Donald Bloxham for sending me pre-publication proofs of the book chapter.

26. Ben Kiernan, *The Pol Pot Regime: Race, Power, and Genocide in Cambodia under the Khmer Rouge 1975–1979*,

3rd ed. (New Haven: Yale University Press, 2008), pp. 460–464.

CHAPTER 2. THE MAKING OF A GENOCIDAIRE

1. Cited in Dmitri Volkogonov, *Stalin: Triumph and Tragedy*, trans. Harold Shukman (New York: Grove Weidenfield, 1991), p. 310.

2. Robert Gellately, *Lenin, Stalin, and Hitler: The Age of Social Catastrophe* (New York: Alfred A. Knopf, 2007), pp. 53–60.

3. Svetlana Alliluyeva, *Twenty Letters to a Friend*, trans. Priscilla Macmillan (New York: Harper and Row, 1967).

4. Martin Malia, "The Soviet Tragedy: A History of Socialism in Russia," in *Stalinism: The Essential Readings*, ed. David Hoffmann (Oxford: Blackwell, 2003), p. 68.

5. Cited in Ronald G. Suny, "Stalin and the Russian Revolution: From Koba to Commissar," manuscript, chap. 1, p. 17. My thanks to Suny for allowing me to read and cite his manuscript.

6. Donald Rayfield, *Stalin and His Hangmen: The Tyrant and Those Who Killed for Him* (New York: Random House, 2004), p. 9.

7. This romanticism emerged later in Stalin's ideas of the heroic in mass mobilization. See David Priestland, "Stalin as Bolshevik Romantic: Ideology and Mobilization, 1917–1939," in *Stalin: A New History*, ed. Sarah Davies and James Harris (Cambridge: Cambridge University Press, 2005), pp. 181–201.

8. Hiroaki Kuromiya, *Stalin: Profiles in Power* (Harlow: Longman, 2005), p. 8.

9. Suny, "Stalin and the Russian Revolution," chap. 1, p. 19.

10. Miklos Kun, *Stalin: An Unknown Portrait* (Budapest, CEU Press, 2003), p. 43.

11. Feliks Chuev, *Tak govoril Kaganovich: Ispoved' stalinskogo apostola* (Moscow, "Otechestva," 1992), p. 81.

12. Norman M. Naimark, "Cold War Studies and New Archival Materials about Stalin," *Russian Review* 61 (January 2002): 11–15.

13. Boris Souvarine, *Stalin: A Critical Survey of Bolshevism* (New York: Longmans, Green, 1939), pp. 224–225.

14. On Lenin, see the introduction to Richard Pipes, ed., *The Unknown Lenin: From the Secret Archive* (New Haven: Yale University Press, 1996), pp. 1, 8, 11. Pipes depicts Lenin as a "heartless cynic" and "a thoroughgoing misanthrope," who had an "utter disregard for human life." He also cites Molotov's assertion that Lenin was "more severe" than Stalin. See also Gellately, *Lenin, Stalin, and Hitler*, pp. 53–57.

15. Jörg Baberowski, *Der Rote Terror: Die Geschichte des Stalinismus* (Munich: Deutsche Verlags-Anstalt, 2003), p. 42.

16. Robert Service, *Stalin: A Biography* (Cambridge: Harvard University Press, 2005), p. 185.

17. Jeremy Smith, *The Bolsheviks and the National Question, 1917–1923* (New York: St. Martin's, 1999), pp. 173–175.

18. See Service, *Stalin*, p. 245.

19. Cited in Simon Sebag Montefiore, *Young Stalin* (New York: Random House, 2007), p. 295.

20. For analyses of the transcripts of the Politburo meetings, see Paul R. Gregory and Norman Naimark, eds., *The Lost Politburo Transcripts: From Collective Rue to Stalin's Dictatorship* (New Haven: Yale University Press, 2009). The Central Committee plenums are available for research in the Hoover Institution archives.

21. Robert C. Tucker, "Foreword," in *Stalin's Letters to Molotov: 1925–1936*, eds. Lars T. Lih, Oleg V. Naumov, and Oleg V. Khlevniuk (New Haven: Yale University Press, 1995), p. xii.

22. Stalin to Molotov [no later than September 15, 1930], in *Stalin's Letters to Molotov*, p. 216.

23. Alfred J. Rieber, "Stalin: Man of the Borderlands," *American Historical Review* 106, 5 (December 2001): 1.

24. Hiroaki Kuromiya, "Stalin in the Light of the Politburo Transcripts," in *The Lost Politburo Transcripts*, eds. Gregory and Naimark, p. 45.

25. Montefiore, *Young Stalin*, p. 268.

CHAPTER 3. DEKULAKIZATION

1. See Andrea Graziosi, *The Great Soviet Peasant War: Bolsheviks and Peasants, 1917–1933* (Cambridge: Harvard University Ukrainian Research Institute, 1996).

2. *Pravda*, February 5, 1931.

3. Cited in Nicolas Werth, "A State against Its People: Violence, Repression, and Terror in the Soviet Union," in *The Black Book of Communism: Crimes, Terror, Repression*, ed. Stephane Courtois et al., trans. Jonathan Murphy (Cambridge: Harvard University Press, 1999), p. 146.

4. Orlando Figes, *The Whisperers: Private Life in Stalin's Russia* (New York: Metropolitan Books, 2007), p. 85.

5. Cited in Mark Iunge, Rol'f Binner, *Kak terror stal "bol'shim": Sekretnyi prikaz No 00447: tekhnologiia ego ispolneniia* (Moscow: Airo-XX, 2003), p. 155.

6. Peter Holquist, "State Violence as Technique: The Logic of Violence in Soviet Totalitarianism," in *Landscaping the Human Garden: Twentieth-Century Population Management in a Comparative Framework*, ed. Amir Weiner (Stanford: Stanford University Press, 2003), p. 145. Quotes from Lynne Viola, *Peasant Rebels under Stalin: Collectivization and the Culture of Peasant Resistance* (New York: Oxford University Press, 1996), p. 37.

7. Cited in Graziosi, *The Great Soviet Peasant War*, p. 49.

8. Paul Hagenloh, *Stalin's Police: Public Order and Mass Repression in the USSR, 1926–1941* (Washington, DC: Woodrow Wilson Center Press, 2009), p. 12.

9. Figes, *The Whisperers*, p. 88.

10. Kuromiya, *Stalin: Profiles in Power*, pp. 91–92.

11. Cited in Lynne Viola, *The Unknown Gulag: The Lost World of Stalin's Special Settlements* (Oxford: Oxford University Press, 2007), p. 155.

12. Ibid., p. 6; Anne Applebaum, *Gulag: A History* (New York: Doubleday, 2003), p. 102.

13. Viola, *The Unknown Gulag*, p. 96.

14. Gellately, *Lenin, Stalin, and Hitler*, p. 227.

15. Nicolas Werth, *Cannibal Island: Death in the Siberian Gulag*, trans. Steven Rendall (Princeton: Princeton University Press, 2007), pp. 76–77

16. Ibid., p. xviii.

17. Vladimir Khaustov and Lennart Samuel'son, *Stalin, NKVD i repressii 1936–1938 gg.* (Moscow: Rosspen, 2009), p. 52.

18. See Hagenloh, *Stalin's Police*, pp. 15, 207; David Shearer, *Policing Stalin's Socialism: Repression and Social Order in the Soviet Union, 1924–1953* (New Haven, Yale University Press, 2009), pp. 313–318. I thank Shearer for sending me a copy of the prepublication page proofs of the book.

19. Marc Jansen and Nikita Petrov, *Stalin's Loyal Executioner: People's Commissar Nikolai Ezhov, 1895–1940* (Stanford: Hoover Institution Press, 2002), p. 91; Khaustov and Samuel'son, *Stalin, NKVD i repressii*, pp. 67–68.

20. Paul Gregory, *Terror by Quota: State Security from Lenin to Stalin* (New Haven: Yale University Press, 2009).

21. Hagenloh, *Stalin's Police*, p. 227.

22. Khaustov and Samuel'son, *Stalin, NKVD, i repressii*, pp. 67–68. Hagenloh doubts the importance of the elections, suggesting instead that Stalin and Yezhov were intent on pursu-

ing "social prophylaxis" to the end, removing all "'threatening' population cohorts in preparation for war." Hagenloh, *Stalin's Police*, p. 285.

23. Wendy Z. Goldman, *Terror and Democracy in the Age of Stalin: The Social Dynamics of Repression* (Cambridge: Cambridge University Press, 2007), p. 128.

24. Amir Weiner, "Introduction," in *Landscaping the Human Garden*, pp. 14–15.

CHAPTER 4. THE HOLODOMOR

1. Conquest, *Harvest of Sorrow: Soviet Collectivization and the Terror-Famine* (New York: Oxford University Press, 1986). For the debates, see the exchange between R. W. Davies and Steven G. Wheatcroft, on the one hand, and Michael Ellman, on the other, in *Europe-Asia Studies* 57, 6 (2005); 58, 4 (2006); and 59, 4 (2007).

2. Kuromiya, *Stalin: Profiles in Power*, p. 103, concludes that 7–8 million died in the Soviet Union and "at least 4 million in Ukraine." Davis and Wheatcroft, as well as Michael Ellman, deal in lower numbers. For example, Ellman uses the figure of 3.2 million who died in Ukraine. Ellman, "Stalin and the Soviet Famine of 1932–33 Revisited," *Europe-Asia Studies*, 59, 4 (2007): 682, n. 30. Ukrainian economic historian Stanislav Kulchytsky estimates that between 3 and 3.5 million people died of starvation and disease (from malnutrition) in the republic itself, but that the total demographic losses, including famine-derived decrease in fertility, was between 4.5 and 4.8 million. See Serhy Yekelchyk, *Ukraine: Birth of a Modern Nation* (New York: Oxford University Press, 2007), p. 112.

3. Nicholas Werth, "Strategies of Violence in the Stalinist USSR," in *Stalinism and Nazism: History and Memory Com-*

148 NOTES TO CHAPTER 4

pared, ed. Henry Russo, trans. Lucy B. Golsan et al. (Lincoln: University of Nebraska Press, 2004), p. 80.

4. See Kuromiya, *Stalin: Profiles in Power*, pp. 111–112.

5. *Stalin's Letters to Molotov*, p. 230, n. 3.

6. Ellman, "Stalin and the Soviet Famine," p. 689.

7. Cited in Terry Martin, *The Affirmative Action Empire: Nations and Nationalism in the Soviet Union, 1923–1939* (Ithaca: Cornell University Press, 2001), p. 301.

8. Nicholas Werth, "The Crimes of the Stalin Regime: Outline for an Inventory and Classification," manuscript, p. 10. My gratitude to Werth for allowing me to cite his manuscript.

9. Martin, *The Affirmative Action Empire*, pp. 306–307.

10. Cited in Gellately, *Lenin, Stalin, and Hitler*, p. 234.

11. See the many testimonies to this effect in *Report to Congress: Commission on the Ukraine Famine* (Washington, DC: U.S. Government Printing Office, 1988), pp. 235–507.

12. See Ellman, "Stalin and the Soviet Famine," pp. 688–689.

13. See Werth, "The Crimes of the Stalin Regime," p. 10.

14. R. W. Davies and Stephen G. Wheatcroft, *The Years of Hunger: Soviet Agriculture 1931–1933* (New York: Palgrave Macmillan, 2004), p. 440.

15. Andrea Graziosi, "The Soviet 1931–1933 Famines and the Ukrainian Holodomor: Is a New Interpretation Possible, and What Would Its Consequences Be?" in *Hunger by Design: The Great Ukrainian Famine and its Soviet Context*, ed. Halyna Hryn (Cambridge: Ukrainian Research Institute, 2008), pp. 3–7.

16. Niccolo Pianciola, "The Collectivization Famine in Kazakhstan, 1931–1933," in ibid., p. 103.

17. See Niccolo Pianciola, "Famine in the Steppe: The Collectivization of Agriculture and the Kazakh Herdsmen, 1928–1934," *Cahiers du Monde russe* 45, 1–2 (2004): 189.

18. Kurt Jonassohn with Karin Solveig Björnson, *Genocide and Gross Human Rights Violations in Comparative Perspective* (New Brunswick, NJ: Transaction Publishers, 1998), p. 256.

CHAPTER 5. REMOVING NATIONS

1. On the "creation" of nationalities, see Ronald G. Suny, *The Revenge of the Past: Nationalism, Revolution, and the Collapse of the Soviet Union* (Stanford: Stanford University Press, 1993).

2. Francine Hirsch, *Empire of Nations: Ethnographic Knowledge and the Making of the Soviet Union* (Ithaca: Cornell University Press, 2005), p. 274.

3. Hoover Institution Archives (hereafter HIA), fond (f.) 17, opis (op.) 2, delo (d.) 591, list (l.) 90; d. 593, l. 79.

4. McLoughlan, "Mass Operations of the NKVD, 1937–38," p. 143.

5. Jansen and Petrov, *Stalin's Loyal Executioner*, pp. 94–95.

6. According to Eric van Ree, Stalin both intensely disliked and reluctantly admired the Poles, an attitude that paralleled his ambivalent admiration and distaste for the Germans. See "Heroes and Merchants: Stalin's Understanding of National Character," *Kritika: Explorations in Russian and Eurasian History* 8, 1 (2007): 49.

7. Khaustov and Samuel'son, *Stalin, NKVD, i repressii*, pp. 29–30; Jansen and Petrov, *Stalin's Loyal Executioner*, pp. 96–99.

8. Jansen and Petrov, *Stalin's Loyal Executioner*, p. 99.

9. Terry Martin, "The Origins of Soviet Ethnic Cleansing," *Journal of Modern History* 70, 4 (December 1998): 857.

10. Pavel Polian, *Against Their Will: The History and Geography of Forced Migration in the USSR* (Budapest: CEU Press, 2004), p. 100.

11. Weiner, "Nothing but Certainty," p. 46.

12. A document sent from Merkulov to Stalin, Molotov, and Beria in May 1941 indicates that the numbers of "anti-Soviet criminal and socially dangerous elements" repressed by the NKVD in the three republics from 1939 to 1941 were somewhat fewer. HIA, f. 89, op. 18, d. 6, l. 1.

13. Polian, *Against Their Will*, pp. 122–123, 167.

14. See Katherine R. Jolluck, *Exile and Identity: Polish Women in Soviet Exile during World War II* (Pittsburgh: Pittsburgh University Press, 2002).

15. Beria recommends the death sentence to Stalin in a communication of March 5, 1940. HIA, f. 89, op. 14, dd. 1–20, l. 9; Zaslavsky, *Class Cleansing*, pp. 32–33.

16. Sarah Meiklejohn Terry, *Poland's Place in Europe: General Sikorski and the Origins of the Oder-Neisse Line* (Princeton: Princeton University Press, 1983), p. 33.

17. A. M. Nekrich, *The Punished Peoples: The Deportation and Fate of Soviet Minorities at the End of the Second World War*, trans. George Saunders (New York: Norton, 1978).

18. Norman M. Naimark, *Fires of Hatred: Ethnic Cleansing in Twentieth Century Europe* (Cambridge: Harvard University Press, 2001), pp. 94–95.

19. Most of the information on the deportation of the Chechens-Ingush and Crimean Tatars is taken from ibid., pp. 94–104.

20. N. F. Bugai, *L. Beriia—I. Stalinu: "Soglasno Vashemu ukazaniiu"* (Moscow: AIRO-XX, 1995).

21. Werth, "The Crimes of the Stalin Regime," p. 16.

22. See Werth "A State against Its People," p. 223, for related figures. Also Polian, *Against Their Will*, pp. 210–211.

CHAPTER 6. THE GREAT TERROR

1. See the new edition of the work, Robert Conquest, *The Great Terror: A Reassessment* (New York: Oxford University Press, 1990).

2. Baberowski, *Der Rote Terror*, p. 201.

3. See Karl Schlögel's evocative *Terror und Traum: Moskau 1937* (Munich: Carl Hanser Verlag, 2008).

4. Figes, *The Whisperers*, p. 159.

5. Wladyslaw Hedeler, "Ezhov's Scenario for the Great Terror," in McLoughlin and McDermott, eds. *Stalin's Terror*, p. 47.

6. Robert C. Tucker and Stephen F. Cohen, eds., *The Great Purge Trial* (New York: Grosset and Dunlap, 1965), p. xxiii.

7. Cited in Volkogonov, *Stalin: Triumph and Tragedy*, p. 293.

8. HIA, f. 89, op. 48, d. 2, l. 13.

9. Charters Wynn, "The 'Smirnov-Eismont-Tolmachev Affair'," in *The Lost Politburo Transcripts*, eds. Gregory and Naimark, pp. 112–113.

10. Tucker and Cohen, *The Great Purge Trial*, p. xxiii. In a private correspondence, Robert Service makes the important point that Stalin did not have a gross personality disorder, which would normally produce a variety of clinical symptoms of paranoia, like involuntary lapses into passivity.

11. Gregory, *Terror by Quota*, p. 104.

12. Ivo Banac, ed., *The Diary of Georgi Dimitrov 1933–1939* (New Haven: Yale University Press, 2003), p. 65.

13. J. Arch Getty and Oleg V. Naumov paint a portrait of Yezhov as a killer, to be sure, but more controlled, bureaucratic, modest, understated, and "banal," in Hannah Arendt's sense, than the one better known to historians. See their *Yezhov: The Rise of Stalin's "Iron Fist"* (New Haven: Yale University Press, 2008), pp. 212–221.

14. Jansen and Petrov, *Stalin's Loyal Executioner*, p. 116.

15. Getty and Naumov, *Yezhov*, p. 7.

16. Werth, "A State against Its People," p. 190.

17. Hiroaki Kuromiya, *The Voices of the Dead: Stalin's Great Terror in the 1930s* (New Haven: Yale University Press, 2007), p. 2.

18. Jörg Baberowski and Anselm Doering-Manteuffel, "The Quest for Order and the Pursuit of Terror," in *Beyond Totalitarianism: Stalinism and Nazism Compared*, eds. Michael Geyer and Sheila Fitzpatrick (New York: Cambridge University Press,

2009), p. 213; Ronald G. Suny, "Stalin and His Stalinism: Power and Authority in the Soviet Union," in *Stalinism and Nazism: Dictatorships in Comparison*, eds. Ian Kershaw and Moshe Lewin (Cambridge: Cambridge University Press, 1997), p. 50.

19. Werth, "The Crimes of the Stalin Regime," p. 15.

20. HIA, f. 89, op. 48, d. 3, l. 14.

21. HIA, f. 89, op. 48, d. 17, l. 31.

22. Cited in Richard Pipes, *Communism: A History* (New York: Modern Library, 2003), p. 63.

23. Jansen and Petrov, *Stalin's Loyal Executioner*, p. 111.

24. J. Arch Getty and Oleg V. Naumov, eds., *The Road to Terror: Stalin and the Self-Destruction of the Bolsheviks, 1932–1939* (New Haven: Yale University Press, 1999), pp. 130–131.

25. McLoughlan, "Mass Operations of the NKVD," p. 128. Getty and Naumov, *Yezhov*, p. 216. The authors suggest, no doubt correctly, that Stalin "trusted Yezhov's judgment," at least in this period.

26. Jansen and Petrov, *Stalin's Loyal Executioner*, pp. 69–70.

27. Khaustov and Samuel'son, *Stalin, NKVD, i repressii*, pp. 23–24.

28. HIA, f. 89, op. 48, d. 12, ll. 25–26.

29. Oleg Khlevniuk, "The Objectives of the Great Terror," in *Stalinism*, p. 97.

30. Shearer, *Policing Stalin's Socialism*, p. 369.

31. Volkogonov, *Stalin: Triumph and Tragedy*, p. 310.

32. Oleg Khlevniuk, *The History of the Gulag: From Collectivization to the Great Terror*, trans. Vadim A. Staklo (New Haven: Yale University Press, 2004), p. 148.

CHAPTER 7. THE CRIMES OF STALIN AND HITLER

1. Conquest, *The Harvest of Sorrow*, p. 3.

2. Stephane Courtois, "Introduction: The Crimes of Communism," in *The Black Book of Communism*, ed. Courtois et al., p. 9.

3. Conquest, *Reflections on a Ravaged Century*, p. xii.
4. Danilo Kis, *Homo-Poeticus: Essays and Interviews* (New York: Farrar, Straus, Giroux, 1995), p. 126. Thanks to Holly Case for alerting me to these essays.
5. Richard Evans, *In Hitler's Shadow: West German Historians' Attempts to Escape from the Nazi Past* (London: I. B. Tauris, 1989), p. 88.
6. Schabas, *Genocide in International Law*, p. 9.
7. Michael Mann, *The Dark Side of Democracy: Explaining Ethnic Cleansing* (Cambridge: Cambridge University Press, 2005), p. 17; Jacques Semelin, *Purify and Destroy: The Political Uses of Massacre and Genocide* (London: Hurst, 2007), pp. 316–320.
8. Eric D. Weitz, *A Century of Genocide: Utopias of Race and Nation* (Princeton: Princeton University Press, 2003), pp. 100–101.
9. Bernd Bonwetsch, "Der GULAG und die Frage des Völkermords," in *Moderne Zeiten? Krieg, Revolution und Gewalt im 20. Jahrhundert*, ed. Jörg Baberowski (Göttingen: Vandenhoeck & Ruprecht, 2006), p. 9.
10. Christian Gerlach and Nicolas Werth, "State Violence—Violent Societies," in *Beyond Totalitarianism*, eds. Geyer and Fitzpatrick, p. 138.
11. Paul Hollander, ed., *From the Gulag to the Killing Fields: Personal Accounts of Political Violence and Repression in Communist States* (Wilmington, DE: ISI Books, 2006), pp. 20–24.
12. Saul Friedländer's emphasis on the singular importance of the Nazi perception of the Jewish threat as "active" and ubiquitous helps distinguish their eliminationist policy against the Jews from the policies against other Nazi victims of genocide. Yet this idea of an "active" and "dangerous" target also inevitably draws comparisons to Stalinist genocidal actions against "kulaks" and other "enemies of the people." Saul Friedländer, *The Years of Extermination: Nazi Germany and the Jews 1939–1945* (New York: Harper Collins, 2007), p. xix.

13. *Deti GULAGa. 1918–1956: Dokumenty* (Moscow: Mezhdunarodnyi fond "Demokratija," 2002.)

14. Courtois does state that his formulation should not be seen as detracting "from the unique nature of Auschwitz." "Introduction," in *The Black Book of Communism*, ed. Courtois et al., p. 9.

15. James J. Sheehan, *Where Have All the Soldiers Gone? The Transformation of Modern Europe* (New York: Houghton Mifflin, 2008).

CONCLUSIONS

1. Gerlach and Werth, "State Violence—Violent Societies," *Beyond Totalitarianism*, p. 176

Index

95, 120, 136–37; political use
of, 53–54

Geladze, Ekaterina (Keke), 36
genocide: categories of victims,
question of, 3–5, 16–17,
21–24, 27–29, 132; convention against (*see* U.N. Convention on the Prevention and
Punishment of the Crime of
Genocide); definitional/legal
characteristics of, 10, 25–28;
examples of (*see* dekulakization; Great Terror, the; nationalities; Ukrainian famine
(the Holodomor); Lemkin's
definition of, 15–17; lives lost
in mass killings of the Stalin
regime, 131–32; need to face,
8; scholarly abstention from
using the word, 124; scholarly dangers confronted in
the study of Soviet, 13–14;
Stalin's crimes and the Holocaust, question of equivalence
of, 2, 121–23, 125–30, 137;
Stalin's mass murders as, 1–2,
123–24; Stalin's mass murders as, inhibitions to making
the argument for, 2–8; torture
and, 114
"Georgian Affair," 80
Germans: Stalin's ambivalence
regarding, 149n.6; as target
of Soviet campaign against
nationalities, 81–82, 84–87
Germany: the Holocaust (*see*

Holocaust, the); Nazi, "working toward the Führer" in,
110; Nazi operation against
the Poles, 91
Goldman, Wendy, 68
Gorky, Maxim, 59
Great October Revolution,
42–43, 51–52
Great Terror, the: atmosphere
and life during, 99–100; end
of, 88; as genocide, 109, 136;
the nationalities, impact on,
84–85, 86–87, 118–19; over-
zealousness by local officials,
110–11; preparations for the
show trials, 103–6; reasons
for and effects of, 116–20;
secrecy and publicity, mixture
of in extraordinary processes,
111–12; the show trials,
18–19, 100–2; Stalin and
Yezhof in charge of, 106–9;
torture in, 112–16
Gregory, Paul, 67
Grigorenko, Piotr, 56
Gulag, the. *See* Archipelago
Gulag

Hagenloh, Paul, 146–47n.22
Hedeler, Wladislaw, 101
Himmler, Heinrich, 128
Hitler, Adolf, 2, 5, 91, 120, 122,
129–30, 137
Hollander, Paul, 125–28
Holocaust, the: Stalin's crimes
and, comparing claims to
genocide of, 2, 121–23,

NKVD (*cont.*)
the Great Terror carried out
by, 111, 117–20; Katyn massacre by, 20, 90–91; the Poles,
campaign against, 85–86;
social cleansing campaigns by,
66–68; torture by, 112–15;
Yagoda, replacement and
purging of, 104, 107
Nuremberg trials, 17–20, 91–92

October (Russian) Revolution,
42–43, 51–52
OGPU (United State Political
Administration): arrests of
Ukrainian peasants during
the famine, 73; data reports
from, veracity of, 11–12; the
kulak problem, reports and
actions regarding, 56–61,
66–67
"On the National Question"
(Stalin), 80
Operation Tannenberg, 91
Order 00447, 67–68, 110,
134

Passov, Z. I., 139–40n.3
passportization campaign, 65
peasants: during the Civil War
and the New Economic Policy,
52–53; the problem of, 51;
during the revolution, 51–52;
solidarity among *vs.* image of
the "kulak," 55–56; Stalin's
actions against (*see*
dekulakization)

People's Commissariat for Internal Affairs. *See* NKVD
Piatakov, Georgy, 101, 103
Pipes, Richard, 144n.14
Poland: Katyn massacre,
20, 91–92; Nazi operation
against, 91
Poles: anti-Polonism, 92; attacks against during World
War II, 89–93 (*see also* Katyn,
massacre of Polish officers
at); Stalin's ambivalence
regarding, 149n.6; as target
of Soviet campaign against
nationalities, 81–82, 84–87,
135
Polish-Soviet War of 1920–21,
45
Pol Pot, 109
purges of 1937-38. *See* Great
Terror, the

Radek, Karl, 101, 103, 105
railway administration, purging
of, 83–84, 119–20
Rayfield, Donald, 9
Roosevelt, Franklin Delano,
16–17
Russian Civil War (1918–1921),
43–44, 52
Russian Revolution (Great
October Revolution), 42–43,
51–52
Rustaveli, Shota, 38
Rykov, Alexey: in the post-Lenin
struggle for power, 47–48;
Stalin's break with, 55; Sta-